WRISTWATCHES

PAOLO DE VECCHI - ALBERTO UGLIETTI

WRISTWATCHES

THE MODELS THAT MADE AN AGE

WHITE STAR PUBLISHERS

© 2005, 2009 Istituto Geografico De Agostini S.p.A., Novara
© 2012 De Agostini Libri S.p.A., Novara

WS White Star Publishers®
is a registered trademark belonging
to De Agostini Libri S.p.A.

© 2014 De Agostini Libri S.p.A.
Via G. da Verrazano, 15
28100 Novara, Italy
www.whitestar.it - www.deagostini.it

Translation: Contextus s.r.l., Pavia, Italy (Sarah Elizabeth Cree)
Editing: Contextus s.r.l., Pavia, Italy

ISBN 978-88-544-0811-1
1 2 3 4 5 6   18 17 16 15 14

Printed in Poland

This book about horology is a work that tells the story of the invention and development of the wristwatch.

The first section focuses on the centrality of the timepiece in everyday life, with special emphasis on the social impact this instrument has had on modern Western civilization, following a centuries-long path that, thanks to increasingly advanced industrialization, led the measurement of time from bell towers to domestic interiors and, finally, the wrist.

The central section is instead dedicated to the top watchmaking brands, names that captivate us with their manufacturing ingenuity and aesthetic acumen. Both characteristics that have contributed to generating an intense and deeply-rooted passion in an increasingly vast number of collectors, who ably and attentively follow developments in the industry, celebrating the rarity but also the innovative charge of models designed over the years by the various manufacturing houses.

It is a history told through the business dynamics of fifty-five world famous brands, most of which are still active today, in clear confirmation of the industry's vitality. The splendid watches illustrated in this volume testify to the ceaseless technological and design progress made between the pioneering period in the early twentieth century to arrival at full maturity in the 1950s and 60s, continuing on to the advent of quartz in the 1970s and 80s up to the powerful return of a passion for mechanics after the year 2000.

High complication models, watches with a basic style and those resulting from technological and/or design experimentation that make up the roll call of greats, including the Patek Philippe Calatrava, the Audemars Piguet Royal Oak, the Cartier Santos and Tank and the Rolex Submariner. Not to forget the colorful Swatch watches, for an overview where plastic and innovative materials are matched with the preciousness of diamonds and gold.

The glossary and bibliography at the end of the volume allow the reader to embark on this long journey through the universe of timepieces armed with the basic concepts of horology.

The authors of this book have included some of the latest models and some of the newest brands and leaders of fresh directions in watchmaking, sadly without being able to mention all of them. But this is only an issue of space and we hope that such names as Graham (illustrated on this page), Greubel Forsey, Hautlance, Jaquet Droz, Moser, Perrelet and Van Cleef & Arpels will, together with many others, find a place in the next editions of this volume.

Contents

From sand to quartz

A mosaic with a representation of a meridian.

A slow evolution

The invention of the mechanical clock, an extraordinary time-measuring machine, is one of humankind's most important achievements, an ideal point of arrival where creative imagination, scientific investigation, technical expertise and aesthetics led to an unprecedented result. The import of the influence of the clock on Western civilization is comparable to that of only a handful of other inventions, including moveable type in the fifteenth century, the steam engine and electricity in the industrial age and the telephone and computer in the twentieth century. When the mechanical clock arrived to take its place in everyday life, the world changed, since it radically

transformed one of fundamental parameters of existence: the concept of time. Time, a supreme and indisputable unit of measure, was from then on no longer determined on the basis of circumstances and natural events, but instead circumscribed by the regular succession of fractions like minutes, hours, days and months. This opened up a new frontier, radically conditioning human activity and fundamentally contributing to the establishment of

Hourglass with a wood and glass structure, European manufacture, eighteenth century.

an urban and civic style that, through continuous evolution over the centuries, became one of the dominant models of modern society. The clock was thus a revolutionary invention, as much for the anthropological implications that typified its development as for the complete self-sufficiency of the mechanical device, an unescapable characteristic of the clock: the energy it requires can be easily replenished through certain components, weights or a mainspring, that permit the movement to run continuously, even at night and in adverse weather

An astrolabe, an ancient portable instrument designed to calculate the height of the sun and another star.

conditions. Its operation is completely unrelated to the instruments that preceded it, sundials and hourglasses, which were explicitly dependent, respectively, on light and the continuous passage of sand. It was an epoch-changing turn that took place in the first half of the last millennium, involving the contribution of all of the most culturally advanced states in medieval Europe. From that point forward, the mechanisms of turret clocks made it possible to mark the hours, displayed on large faces decorating churches and public buildings and often complemented by devices that provided an acoustic announcement of time through the interaction of bell hammers set into motion by complicated mechanisms and different kinds of bells,

Personal timepiece, United Kingdom, seventeenth century.

sonorously marking out the events of community life, regulated by the ecclesiastic or civic authorities. Mechanical horology satisfied the ever-greater need for precision and reliability necessary for

Weight-driven "lantern" clock, Italy, sixteenth century.

keeping pace with developments in the Western world and was also possessed of enormous potential for technological development, linked to the possibility of constantly updating the characteristics of the movement. Among the most important innovations, we should cite the progressive research dedicated to miniaturizing the mechanism, which contributed to making the clock portable, releasing it from the 'public' posting of time and bringing the information into the 'private' sphere. The clock's use in domestic space was followed by its personal use: initially worn around the neck or kept in a special pouch, it later found a secure place in the pockets of elegant men's waist-coats in the nineteenth century

and, finally, came to be worn on the wrist. The latter fashion made a critical contribution to the widespread diffusion of the watch, which over the course of the years assumed a multiplicity of meanings, going beyond simple utility to becoming a status symbol and one of the most firmly established indicators of personal taste and fashion trends: but this is already twentieth century history. The world of clocks elevates the manufacturing primacy of Europe through its watchmakers—flanked by great scientists—who have risen to take on a gripping and unique challenge, marked by the drive to improve the technology applied to timepieces and refine their construction technique. Sometimes they have been inspired by extreme circumstances, like in the case of the Campani brothers, artisans

A horology workshop in a miniature in the De Sphaera codex, Ambrogio De Predis, 1480.

Lantern clock, Italy, seventeenth century.

active in Rome in the seventeenth century who designed the 'notturni', clocks that displayed the time at night by projecting a rotating and graduated barrel illuminated by a small copper oil lamp set inside the case; the gearing of these clocks was completely silent and utterly lacking in the classic tick-tock of the mechanism. All to satisfy the needs of Pope Alexander VII, who slept poorly at night. It is a history defined by adventurous episodes, rich in emotional tension, initially set in Italy, Germany, France and England, with Switzerland taking the lead in more recent times and today synonymous with the highest levels of horologic quality and precision. It is a tradition marked by masterpieces of unsurpassed beauty, the fruit of a 'organizational miracle' that manifested all of its potential utilizing a truly extraordinary chain of production, almost exclusively tied to human talent, an inseparable factor of the success of an industry in which creativity has always played a central role. Whether a matter of complex mechanisms or purely aesthetic finishing touches is of little importance: the timepiece is the only machine still used in our society that, although being transformed by futuristic materials and fresh solutions, still maintains the same structural architecture used by the original movements in a by now distant age. This fact further exalts the magnificent invention of the unknown and brilliant artisan who first dreamed up the clock, a fascinating, wondrous instrument that lends a magical aspect to the passage of time.

Table clock, Germany, sixteenth century.

The birth of the mechanics of time

The first mechanical clocks date to the early Middle Ages. Scholars agree that the invention of the mechanical clock is linked to the monastic practice of ringing a bell to call monks to prayer. Primitive devices were used in monasteries and abbeys all over Europe to sound a bell at various times of day to announce periods of prayer and work ("ora et labora", as expressed in the famous Benedictine Rule), marking the day of the monks. Not so much a clock, this

Astronomical clock, Prague, fifteenth century.

instrument was a time marker, precisely like sundials and hourglasses. But the extraordinary merit of these monastic devices was that they worked using an actual mechanism, even if a rudimentary one. Be that as it may, even outside the rigid monastic world, around the year one thousand, the need began to arise for tools that could help organize an increasingly complex social life. And it was precisely for this reason that the first true clocks were public ones (the personal timepiece would be a later conquest): large in size, they were set up on bell towers, so that people could see and hear them even from a distance, in the city streets and the surrounding countryside. Turret clocks, among other things, precisely corresponded to the social organization of the age. Everything depended on the local authority, and so, from both the practical and symbolic points of view, it was logical for time to be marked off on buildings of power. A number of European countries claim to have built the first and most important public clocks. Based on the available documentation, historians venture the following dates: 1258, Chartres Cathedral (France); 1282, Exeter Cathedral, (England); 1286, St Paul's Cathedral,

London; 1292, Canterbury (England) and Sens (France) Cathedrals; 1306, the church of Sant'Eustorgio, Milan. At the time, they must have been seen as extraordinary machines and it would not be mistaken to think that they represented a tangible sign of a city's power. Their structure consisted of a large iron cage and their operation was ensured by a wheelwork, a series of moving wheels connected to the clock hands and bells and put into motion by the tractive force of weights. The 'constancy' of this force was essential (and in fact guaranteed by the laws of gravity), but it was just as critical to trigger a rhythm that would in some way represent a unit of measurement (the classic tick-tock): toward this end, two devices were developed, the 'escapement' and the 'regulator', that transformed the continuous movement supplied by the driving force of the weights into an intermittent movement. It is extraordinary to consider that, from that time to the present day, the operational theory behind mechanical clocks has remained virtually unchanged. Development has focused on the constant improvement of materials, the challenge of reducing the size of the various components and the substitution of the driving force of the weights with that supplied by a metal spring. This was an important step for bringing clock faces down from towers and into private homes (and then into pockets and, finally, onto the wrist). But arriving at the 'domestic' marking of time was not only a matter

of technology. It also represented the rise of a new way of thinking, the direct consequence of social and economic changes in fifteenth-century Europe. The pivotal factor was the unstoppable expansion of the concept of 'private'. The possibility of knowing the time (to a more or less precise degree, considering that more than five hundred years ago, deviations that would be intolerable today were then acceptable) within the walls of a home, workshop or public institution was a matter of

Finely decorated clock in gilt bronze, Germany, seventeenth century.

historical significance. No longer depending on 'public' time or empirical measurements tied to natural phenomena was a shift that decisively opened the way to the social organization that led to (pre- and post-) industrial civilization as we know it today. While from the technical point of view, the first domestic clocks were nothing more than miniaturized turret clocks. Their structure in

Night clock, Italy, seventeenth century.

fact consisted of a metal cage open on three sides with a brass face on the fourth side. Often, they were topped by a bell, which was struck by a clapper to sound the hour. They were first produced in the fifteenth century in Germany and England, where they were called, respectively, 'Gothic' and 'lantern' clocks (in the latter case, the etymology would seem to be directly connected to their shape). They were driven by the gravitational force of weights, for which reason they were hung on a hook on the wall or set on special shelves.

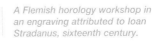

A Flemish horology workshop in an engraving attributed to Ioan Stradanus, sixteenth century.

Domestic time

A pendulum mantle clock in walnut, Naples, eighteenth century.

The decisive step toward the 'personal' use of time was made when (once again, the invention cannot be traced to a single individual) the driving force of weights (which was effective but inconvenient and awkward) was replaced by a more advanced form of energy. This innovation took the name 'spring'. It was a slender strip of wrought brass (a material that was later replaced by tempered steel) that, after being coiled around a fixed element (wound with a key) inside a special cylindrical container (the barrel), turned and so supplied energy to the mechanism. With the burden of weights literally removed, clockmakers (essentially blacksmiths with more skill and talent than their colleagues) were free to imagine the individual 'portability' of timekeepers, a direction with far greater implications than their simple and already common 'transportability' from one room to another in buildings. The oldest securely documented spring clock dates to 1450 (probably a modified weight model) and came from Germany (Augsburg and Nuremburg were the main production centers), but France (specifically, Flanders and Burgundy) shares the distinction for producing some of the earliest domestic clocks. With this new function also came aesthetic renovation: the most interesting aspects concern the containment of the measures, the application of additional faces or decorated surfaces, which came to completely enclose the mechanisms, and the places where the objects were kept: on tables, furniture and fireplaces. The most common types were Tabernacle Clocks and

Clock in the form of a birdcage with a singing bird automaton, Pierre Jacquet-Droz, 1785.

Table Clocks (with a horizontal face and circular base), but there were also parallelepipeds with a hexagonal or four-sided base. The spring proved itself to be the perfect solution for the development of portable horology. But what worked magnificently in theory was not equally effective in its practical application. The spring in fact had the unpardonable defect of starting out with a great deal of speed and then moving very slowly toward the end. This fact, which was further complicated by the artisans' incomplete mastery of the materials, was exactly contrary to the need for energy constancy.

The problem with tension was resolved through the development of regulation devices (the most common were the fusee and the stackfreed): connected to the barrel, they ensured the regular dispensation of the driving force supplied by the spring. At this point, one can say that the clock, once all of the problems connected to the miniaturization of the various elements were resolved, had all its cards in place for becoming truly portable. 'Personal', therefore: precious pendant models for ladies and pocket versions for gentlemen. This does not at all mean that all of the research previously carried out on 'stationary' clocks was abandoned. It simply means that the two types, at a certain point, took two parallel paths, each leading to considerable results in technology for measuring time and the aesthetics of its representation.

Group of pendulum table clocks in gilt brass, France, nineteenth century.

The search for precision

During the seventeenth century, Italy and the Netherlands were each home to one of the most captivating and important innovations toward the achievement of the greatest possible precision in horology at the time. This was the pendulum regulator, an application of the Italian astronomer Galileo Galilei's research on the isochrony of the oscillations of a body suspended at the end of a thread. Both Galileo Galilei (in 1637) and the Dutch mathematician Christiaan Huygens (in 1656, presumably neither knowing about the other's work), thought of using the symmetrical precision of the pendulum's oscillations to mark time. Equipped with springs and pendulum adjustment instead of weights and balance adjustment, it was now possible to devise a new generation of timekeepers. The new instruments were far more precise than their predecessors, passing immediately from a deviation of between 15 and 30 minutes to around 30 seconds per day. The pendulum thus became used for a wide range of clocks in various places throughout Europe up to and throughout the nineteenth century.

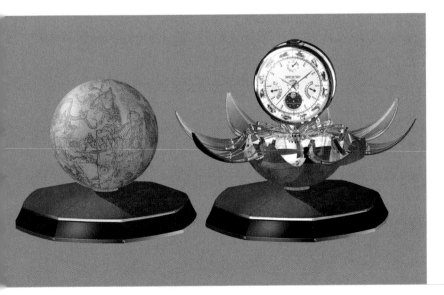

A singular episode

A special chapter in the history of the search for precision is dedicated to the challenge presented by longitude. This was a venture that, from the beginning of the seventeenth century until the first half of the eighteenth century, involved the most powerful navies of the time: those of England and Spain first and foremost, but also those of France, the Netherlands, Genoa and Venice. The problem was no small affair, since having the precise longitude and latitude was necessary to calculating a route. The latter (a position north or south of the equator) was relatively simple to calculate. The problems were presented by the former (a position east or west of a reference meridian). The vital importance of the precise identification of longitude (in an age when sea voyages were not only undertaken to make new geographical discoveries but also for the acquisition of wealth and power) becomes crystal clear when one considers that miscalculating the equator by a single degree would take a ship off course by more than one hundred kilometers. It was widely believed among high-ranking naval officers that one could obtain precise calculations of longitude by bringing onboard a clock capable of precisely calculating the hour of the reference meridian compared with that of the local one. The wager was won by the English, thanks to the ingenuity of the horologist John Harrison, who found himself having to compete with the best minds of the age (the conclusive test took place in 1759): his fellow Englishmen Arnold and Earnshaw, the French Le Roy and Ferdinand Berthoud (although born in Switzerland) and the Dutch Huygens. At this point, it would not be at all rash to conclude that the English navy became as powerful as it did in part due to the exceptional clocks they used onboard

Esprit des Cabinotiers, the "synthesis" of horology according to Vacheron Constantin, a unique piece produced in 2005 for the foundation's 250th anniversary.

their ships. Be that as it may, the pendulum regulator suffered from the oscillations of the ship. In fact, the next most celebrated timekeeper used for sea navigation was the marine chronometer, which was worked out in its initial form by the English clockmaker Sir Thomas Earnshaw in the second half of the eighteenth century. This instrument had a balance adjustment device, spring detent escapement, a power reserve indicator and, most importantly, a cardan suspension for the cylindrical brass case (resistant to corrosion) that would keep the device horizontal at all times regardless of the rolling and pitching of the ship. Housed in a mahogany and brass travel case, the marine chronometer underwent constant improvement and remained essential for navigation up to the arrival of satellite navigation.

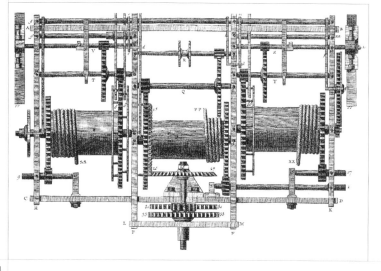

An illustration of a horology mechanism in Diderot and d'Alembert's encyclopedia, 1765.

Inventions and innovations

A pair of watches decorated with multicolor enamel and made to mirror one another, Switzerland, eighteenth century.

Another development that was fundamental to the invention of modern horology concerns, this time, a specific individual. This individual was Abraham-Louis Breguet (1747–1823), considered by far the most brilliant and prolific horologist of his time. Born in Neuchâtel to a Protestant family of French origin, after an apprenticeship at the court of Versailles he opened, around 1775, his own workshop in Paris, on Quai de l'Horloge. His business depended on more than one hundred employees, many of whom were top-rank artisans and scientists. A technological genius who developed a highly individual style, Abraham-Louis Breguet achieved a level of personal fame unique in the entire history of horology, due to the excellence and originality of his timepieces, characterized by daring mechanical complications and an aesthetic style for cases and faces as imaginative as it was rigorous. His customers, who immediately also became prestigious endorsers, included the crowned sovereigns of all of Europe as well as aristocrats, the well-to-do and high officials of the age. The Duke of Wellington and Napoleon himself owned only Breguet timepieces. The sheer number and quantity of Abraham-Louis Breguet's inventions and improvements—technical and aesthetic—is extraordinary. Here are a few examples. The perpetual timepiece, or self-winding. The employment of jewels to reduce friction in the mechanisms. The definitive perfection of the repeater, or rather the system for striking the hours and minutes on command. The perpetual calendar, a mechanical memory that automatically indicates the date, day, month, year (including Leap Year) and lunar phases. The tourbillon, a balance adjustment device that neutralizes the differences in position experienced by the watch in its everyday use. The faces designed by Breguet are distinguished for their "à guilloché" decoration, done entirely by hand, and for their harmoniously off-center indicators. Even the clock hands were lavished with special care, and are distinctive for their circumference and pointed ends. While the cases are true works of the jeweler's art, with "cannelé" decoration along the caseband. These characteristics have remained mostly unchanged even in the models produced by the watch manufacturing house that inherited Breguet's name and tradition.

Gold and multicolor enamel pocket watch, Switzerland, nineteenth century.

Increasingly portable

Discussion of Abraham-Louis Breguet also presents an opportunity to recall another fascinating object type that has carved out a place for itself in the endless literature on timepieces. Curiously, collectors and those in the profession call these particular clocks "pendules d'officier" or "pendules de voyage" (officer's or travel pendulum clocks), despite the fact that they employ balance, rather than pendulum, adjustment. Their definitive development was the fruit of another of Breguet's brilliant ideas, who in effect invented a new and exceedingly useful kind of timekeeper. Although fully transportable (kept inside a special padded carrying case) and small in size, they were equipped with

all of the technical features common to larger, sophisticated table clocks (a range of striking mechanisms, an eight-day duration and an alarm). Always made of gilt brass with glass sides displaying the mechanism, these clocks usually had a cube-shaped or round case and

Gold and pearl pocket watch, Switzerland, eighteenth century.

were always provided with a handle for transport. According to tradition, the name "pendules d'officier" stems from their wide-scale adoption by high French officers during the Napoleonic Campaigns. For the record, one should add that other travel timekeepers had been invented previous to these, with completely different characteristics and uses than the "pendules d'officier". Their name, "carriage clocks", is deceiving, suggesting that they were used by aristocrats and high prelates while travelling. But this is highly improbable, given travel conditions centuries ago. Their shape having been directly borrowed from pocket models, but with large cases usually made in wrought silver, these clocks probably took their name from the fact that they were designed to be easily transported in their special wood or precious leather carrying cases. Lavishly decorated and equipped with a range of striking mechanisms, when the journey was completed, their aristocratic owners could use them throughout their stay away from home.

Carriage clock with case, European manufacture, seventeenth century.

The triumph of horology

Gold watch with calendar, lunar phases and power reserve, A. L. Breguet, nineteenth century.

The nineteenth century saw the rise of the pocket watch, which was the launch pad for the wristwatch, which would be in turn the extraordinary invention of the twentieth century. (And which would be in the early stages, and not by chance, simply a waistcoat pocket watch adapted to be worn on the left wrist.) Pocket watches emerged during a period when timepieces had already become widely popular. This was in part because they were increasingly necessary to everyday life, and in part because by then they were being produced by real industrial manufacturers, which guaranteed the production of formidable quantities and a wide range of prices. No longer limited to the elite, the timepiece also changed its primary production area: England, France, Germany and Italy waned, while the United States and, most of all, Switzerland came to the fore. It was in fact the Confederation that took the lead in terms of the quality and quantity of timepieces produced, a position that would be further entrenched when pocket models made way for wristwatches. This was also the period during which brands still active on the market today began manufacturing their products. Or, in some cases, they simply successfully continued their pro-

Gold watch with perpetual calendar, Audemars Piguet.

duction, like Vacheron & Constantin, which was founded in Geneva in 1755 and is the oldest manufacturer among those whose activity has continued uninterrupted. But the road that would lead the watch from waistcoat pockets to the wrists of men and women in a society barreling towards "modernity" was made up (and could not have been otherwise) of a whole series of technical and stylistic innovations. One of the most important of which was the invention of the winding crown by the firm Patek Philippe, another historic name in Swiss horology. This milestone dates to the second half of the nineteenth century and was, with the definitive elimination of the use of a special key, the first sign of the impending wristwatch revolution. A type of watch that was in a certain sense required, or at least favored, by the new, more dynamic lifestyle of the twentieth century, but one that was also directly influenced by fashion, which in those years was changing the way everyone dressed, abandoning the by then antiquated clothing of the past.

The famed "Marie Antoinette" watch, A. L. Breguet, 1783–1827.

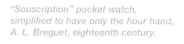

"Souscription" pocket watch, simplified to have only the hour hand, A. L. Breguet, eighteenth century.

Time for the modern world

A marine chronometer with a wooden case and cardan suspension, London, 1858.

Around 1900, everything changed. Trains, airplanes, ocean liners and automobiles all came on the scene. And pocket watches became a thing of the past. The dynamics of use that led to this epoch-changing evolution are suggested in a few theories about how the wristwatch emerged (while interesting, none of these theories have been proven). A few scholars imagine that it all began with an anonymous nanny, who found it more convenient to use a measuring tape to secure her watch to her wrist than let it hang dangerously from her bodice. There is also a male theory, which traces the origins of the wristwatch to the solutions thought up at Girard-Perregaux (as well as Omega and Eberhard) in response to officers' requests: modern warfare did not allow looking in one's pocket for one's indispensable timepiece, instead requiring the quick glance that only a watch strapped to a wrist would permit. The more aristocratic thesis instead concerns the great Louis Cartier, who was apparently asked by his friend and aviation pioneer Alberto Santos-Dumont in 1904 to design a watch as extremely elegant as it was convenient to consult. However it came to pass, what clearly emerges from all of these theories is that the necessary condition for

the success of the wristwatch had everything to do with the concept of "practicality", flanked by the decorative appearance, insomuch as "jewelry". In fact, the first historically documented wristwatch was a lady's model: dated 1868, it was commissioned from Patek Philippe by the Hungarian Countess Koscowicz, for whom the watchmaker created a gold and diamond bracelet with a hidden dial. But even though the horology tradition had centuries of experience in the areas of decoration and working with metals and precious stones, enamel and chasing,

One of the countless variations of the Jaeger-LeCoultre Atmos pendulum clock, based on Jean-Léon Reutter's invention.

in the realm of practicality and elegance on the wrist, the whole road still lay ahead. And it was certainly not enough to simply move the winding and adjustment crown from twelve o'clock to three o'clock (with the addition of bars attached to the case for securing the strap). Instead it was a matter of continuous technical and stylistic innovation, and involved all of the big "Swiss Made" companies. It was again Cartier to shine, experimenting in the early twentieth century with a four-sided design for the cases of its Santos and Tank models, contemporary versions of which are still being produced today and which launched the category of non-circular watches. With the Reverso model (1931), Jaeger-LeCoultre patented the swivel case, a solution for protecting the dial that was also epoch-making in aesthetic terms. Earlier, in 1929,

Riefler precision regulator clock, Germany, 1922.

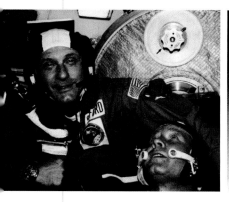

Jaeger-LeCoultre had stunned the world of watches with the extreme miniaturization of its Due Linee movement (with a weight of one gram and measuring 4.85 x 14 millimeters), which was perfect for creating sophisticated pieces that were as much watches as jewelry. Patek Philippe underlined its own aristocratic nature with the elegance of the Calatrava model (1932), which immediately became one of the great classics. Rolex, just a few years after its founding and immediately positioning itself as a cutting-edge sports brand, presented its first Oyster model in 1926, with its groundbreaking watertight case. A characteristic that, together with the perfecting of the automatic movement (the Perpetual system of 1931, which had a two-direction central rotor, following the experimental models Harwood, Rolls and Wig-Wag) ensured Rolex primacy in "modernity". 1950 saw the widespread circulation of the classic models and the successful application to wristwatches of the full range of mechanical "complications" previously developed for nineteenth-century pocket watches. In the 1960s, Piaget reached its apex, presenting sophisticated extra-thin watches for men and women's models that were like Baroque sculptures for the wrist. Those were also the years of space exploration, and Breitling's Cosmonaute and Omega's

Speedmaster chronographs became the official watches of NASA astronauts. Science fiction became reality and on the wave of this thrilling achievement, the focus turned to technological and design developments that were previously unimaginable. And now the American-made electronic watches stepped onto the stage: The Hamilton Ventura, with its asymmetrical case, the Bulova Accutron, with its transparent face revealing its electronic workings, and the Hamilton Pulsar, with its rounded dial and digital display. After 1970, a new chapter began, and the advent of quartz electronic watches and the new economic front opened up by Japanese production put the Swiss timepiece industry in temporary difficulty. It recovered in 1983 with the launch of Swatch ("Swiss Watch") watches, which, with a vast range of designs and high-tech production, ushered in a new way of understanding and collecting watches. The new frontier will be wrist models that, like real terminals, function as portable telephones, databases, personal computers and satellite navigators. But here we are looking to the future and by now the full range of twentieth-century horology has become the stuff of collections.

A colorful array of Swatch watches, symbol of twenty-first century watchmaking innovation founded on use of plastic materials and electronic technology.

The Brands

Lange 1A

Watch with outsize date, off-center display of hours and minutes, yellow gold case, gold dial and some mechanism components in gold. Limited series of 100 pieces, 1998.

A Saxon manufacture of noble origins and with a tradition of technical excellence, after suffering from the events following the Second World War and the consequential division of Germany, it returned to the fore in the 1990s.

A. Lange & Söhne

To tell the story of A. Lange & Söhne, a prestigious German horology company, we need to travel back to golden age of Saxony and in particular its capital, Dresden, starting in the reign of Augustus the Strong, a sovereign who, in the final years of the seventeenth century, brought a refined taste and passion for the arts and sciences to his court. This dynamic and creative context was maintained until the nineteenth century, when Saxony became the birthplace of a fertile generation of horologists, including Johann Christian Friedrich Gutkaes and Ferdinand Adolph Lange.

The A. Lange & Söhne building in a vintage photo.

1815 Up and Down

Watch with power reserve indicator, rose gold case, crocodile strap.

Langematik

Watch with outsize date and self-winding mechanism, yellow gold case, baton indices.

Tourbillon Pour le Mérite

Manual-winding tourbillon, power reserve indicator, yellow gold case. Limited series of 50 pieces in platinum, 150 in gold and 1 in steel, 1994.

Langematik Perpetual

Perpetual calendar with outsize date and self-winding mechanism, yellow gold case.

The latter, after studying with Gutkaes and in Paris in the atelier of Winnerl, who was famous for the structural quality of his chronometers, set out to pursue his own entrepreneurial path. In 1845, in order to overcome the profound crisis then affecting the area of the Ore Mountains, Lange proposed the creation of a workshop dedicated to teaching the art of horology in Glasütte, a town in the center of that zone. With a loan from the Interior Ministry, his adventure began, together with a centuries-long history based on top-level technical performance. The manufacturing business remained a family affair: the founding of A. Lange & Söhne in 1868 in fact marked the entry of the founder's son, Richard, into the company, followed three years later by his brother Emil.

Double Split

Chronograph with a double-rattrapante function (one for minutes, one for seconds), manual-winding, with a platinum case.

Günter Blümlein

Lange 1 Tourbillon

Manual-winding tourbillon, outsize date and indication of power reserve, with a platinum case. Limited series of 150 platinum pieces and 250 in rose gold, 2000.

Datograph

Manual-winding chronograph with a platinum case and a crocodile strap.

Around 1930, A. Lange & Söhne began producing wristwatches, but the history of the manufacturing house suffered an abrupt halt in 1945. On May 8, the main building was destroyed by bombing. This was the first of a serious of devastating events for A. Lange & Söhne, which lost its position as a manufacturer for the elite upon the nationalization of the company (1948) and its subsequent entry into a state consortium,

Anniversary Langematik

Self-winding watch with a platinum case and enamel dial, limited edition of 500 pieces, 2000. Below, a detail of the dial.

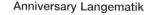

the Glashütter Uhrenbetriebe. These were painful transitions, which marked Saxony's passage under the socialist regime. On December 7, 1990, after forty years of sorrowful oblivion, Walter Lange, representing the fourth generation of the family of horologists from Glashütte, stepped into the limelight: with the help of

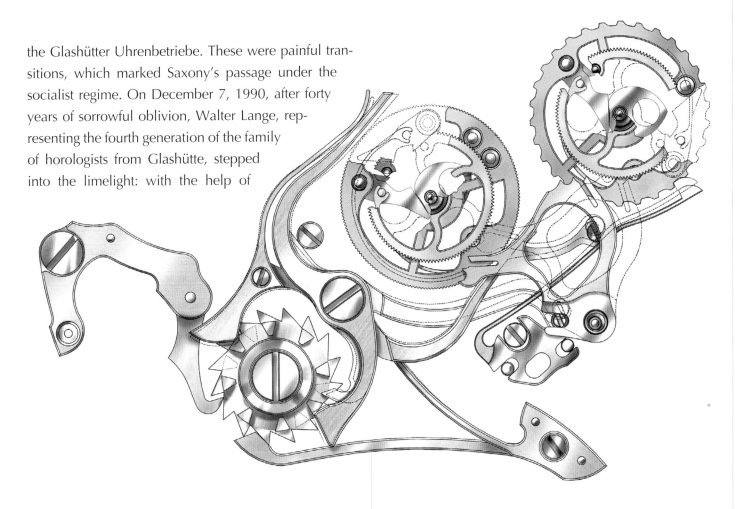

Günter Blümlein, an enlightened manager responsible for the horology division of the Mannesmann Group, the fairy tale of A. Lange & Söhne was reborn. Since 2000, the company has been a part of Richemont, a luxury multinational. Four years after its re-founding, the Lange 1 appeared on the market: timepiece enthusiasts celebrated the return of the German watch manufacturer and the new model was a considerable success. Other masterpieces followed, including the Tourbillon Pour le Mérite, the only wrist model with a winding system inherited from marine chronometers and the most precious pocket watches; the Langematik, with a self-winding mechanism and a gold and platinum rotor; the Datograph and the Langematik Perpetual, respectively a chronograph and perpetual calendar of rare beauty and quality and, finally, the Double Split, a chronograph with a double-rattrapante (split second) function.

A drawing showing the mechanism of the Lange Double Split, a chronograph of tremendous structural complexity. Below, the Lange caliber L00.1, the manual-winding mechanism of the Double Split, made up of 465 components.

The development of technical performance continued its forward march: the perpetual winding device was introduced in the Tourbograph and other models, for which the denomination "Pour le Mérite" indicates application of that technology. The Lange 1 became self-winding and was enhanced by the indication of a second time zone, with a peripheral ring marked with the reference cities for the world's twenty-four time zones.

Richard Lange Pour le Mérite

Part of the collection celebrating the 165th anniversary of the brand's founding, this watch has a platinum case and a sapphire glass caseback revealing the manual-winding movement. The series is limited to 50 pieces.

Lange 31

A manual-winding watch with twin barrels, 31-day power reserve, small seconds, date and a 46-millimeter platinum case.

Lange Zeitwerk Striking Time

Manual-winding in white gold with a "jumping numerals" display of hours and minutes, power reserve indicator and quarter-hour and full-hour chiming mechanism.

Tourbograph Pour le Mérite

A rattrapante chronograph with a manual-winding tourbillon and a special fusée-and-chain transmission, the series "Homage to F. A. Lange" commemorates the 165th anniversary of the company's founding and is limited to 50 pieces with a honey gold case.

Cabaret Tourbillon

In rose gold with a manual-winding movement made up of 373 components (84 of which in the tourbillon cage), date indicator, small seconds and a 120-hour power reserve.

But it was with the Zeitwerk, unveiled in 2000 and subsequently produced in numerous editions with precious metal cases, that A. Lange & Söhne stunned industry insiders and conquered connoisseurs of the most sophisticated horology. Through a complex mechanism, the hours and minutes are indicated in two apertures on the dial, with the hours on the left and the minutes displayed symmetrically on the right. This design transferred the digital display of time from monumental clocks, usually used in theaters to announce the start of a show or the acts of an opera, to the wrists of admirers of this new direction for German timepieces.

One of the most celebrated Swiss houses, it is one of the few to boast a high level of production independence. Its fame is founded on its brilliance in producing complicated pocket and wrist models filled with technology and allure. Since 1972, it has dominated the world of luxury sport watches with the Royal Oak, one of the industry's true benchmarks.

Audemars Piguet

udemars Piguet was founded in 1875 in Le Brassus, in the Vallée de Joux, by Edward-Auguste Piguet and Jules-Louis Audemars. The former invested 10,000 Swiss Francs in the enterprise, while the latter contributed eighteen mechanical movements. In 1882, they registered the trademark "Audemars Piguet & Cie" and the house, with Jules handling production and Edward dealing with commercial activity, specialized from the start in manufacturing ultra-thin and complicated watches. Toward the end of the nineteenth century, the Grande Complication pocket watch was unveiled, with perpetual calendar, minute repeater, lunar phase and split-second chronograph functions. Seven years later, Audemars Piguet participated in the International Exposition in Paris: their watches were met with such success that it formed the foundation for ever-greater expansion and Edward Piguet opened sales agencies in London, Berlin, New York, Paris and Buenos Aires.

In the first years of the twentieth century, a new facility was inaugurated and the manufacture continued along its path of research and experimentation, with special attention to improving the minute repeater. The first wrist model featuring this complication was followed a few years later by the announcement of the smallest repeater mechanism in the world, with a diameter of just 15.8 millimeters. In 1924, Audemars Piguet introduced two highly innovative wristwatches: the Complete Calendar, with lunar phases, and the Jump Hour, with hours displayed digitally and a central minute hand. These models constituted the pillars of the company's production, completed by manual-winding chronographs of exceptional technical elegance and a few specialties, which have become part of the house's genetic code. These include the skeleton models, which feature a finely decorated mechanism with bridges and gears carved out to their structural limits for a purely decorative aim, pieces

Audemars Piguet headquarters in Le Brassus.

Opposite:
Ore Universali

Manual-winding watch with an "hours of the world" indicator and yellow gold case, produced in the period when the house opened its agency in Geneva, around 1940.

Minute Repeater

Manual-winding watch with a yellow and white gold case, customized with the name of its owner, John Shaeffer, on the dial, 1907.

Small Seconds

Manual-winding watch
with a yellow gold case
and unusually shaped
horns, circa 1920.

Complete Calendar

Manual-winding watch
with triple date calendar
and a white gold case,
circa 1920.

inaugurated the creation of a new category in the world of timepieces: the sports watch. The designer of the timeless Royal Oak line was Gérald Genta who, in order to guarantee the watertightness of the case, took inspiration from the seal of ship portholes. The clock features two flat gaskets, one between the bezel and the case middle and the other between the case middle and the back cover: the five layers were secured by eight visible screws. The bezel, like the back cover, was octagonal and topped by an elongated hexagonal case completed by an integrated bracelet. It was an absolute novelty for that period, with a high price which led the Royal Oak to be considered the most expensive steel watch in the world at the time and a true status symbol. The Royal Oak line continued to grow, hosting within its case, available in various metals, the full range of complications, proving itself to be the manufacturing house's most successful line in terms of both sales and image.

with sophisticated case designs that privilege an aesthetic reading of the watch and, most of all, extra-thin movements. The manual-winding nine-line ML caliber of 1946, just 1.65 millimeters thick, was joined in the 1960s by the AP2120 caliber with a 21 carat gold central rotor (total thickness: 2.45 millimeters). Three years later, the date version of the same mechanism increased its thickness by a mere 0.60 with respect to the original caliber.

Under the leadership of George Golay, the eclectic head who guided Audemars Piguet production through a major change in direction, the brand's signature watch emerged: the Royal Oak. "One of the best designs of this century. And probably the next one". That was the slogan for a Royal Oak ad campaign in the 1990s, the perfect synthesis of the innovative force of the model which

Skeleton

Manual-winding watch
with a finely skeletonized
movement and a yellow
gold case, 1953.

Tourbillon

Manual-winding watch
with a yellow gold
case and a large
satin-finish bezel,
circa 1950.

Tourbillon

Self-winding watch with a
tourbillon device and yellow
gold case. This was the first
automatic tourbillon wristwatch
ever made, 1986.

Star Wheel

Self-winding watch,
with a yellow gold

case and sector hour
display on numbered
discs, 1991.

Flying Saucer

Manual-winding watch
with "clous de Paris"
pattern on the bezel
and yellow gold case,
circa 1990.

T he company's more traditional production continued along its path of innovation and exclusivity with the launch in 1978 of the automatic perpetual calendar (which was then also applied to the Royal Oak collection), making a decisive contribution to the public's rediscovery of this long-forgotten specialty. 1992 was the year of the Triple Complication, and in 1993, the Royal Oak Offshore was introduced, inaugurating a "family within a family": the debut chronograph had impressive dimensions, taking the classic Royal Oak design to the extreme, further emphasizing its sports connotation. The Offshore was also a market success, strengthened by its endorsement by many top athletes in various sports. 1996 was the year of the Grande Complication wristwatch. This watch had a round case with a 42-millimeter diameter containing an AP2887 caliber made up of six hundred elements that, orchestrated by the talented technicians

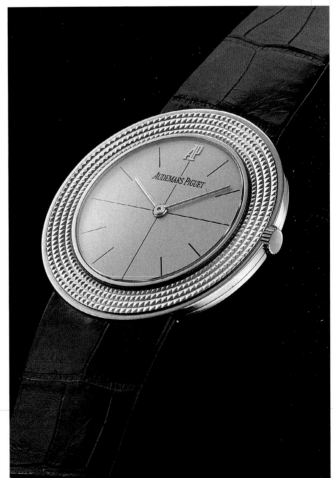

Chronograph

Manual-winding watch with a yellow gold case, circa 1940.

Complete Calendar Chronograph

Manual-winding watch with a yellow and white gold case, circa 1940.

Grande Complication

Self-winding watch with minute repeater, perpetual calendar, week indicator, chronograph with rattrapante hand and a platinum case, 1996.

of Audemars Piguet, combined a perpetual calendar, minute repeater and split second chronograph. It was a masterpiece produced in only five pieces per year, a limit imposed by the enormous difficulty of its manufacture.

Among the house's more recent lines, one should certainly mention those named in memory of the company founders: the Jules Audemars has an elegant, round case and comes in versions featuring complications like equation of time, perpetual calendar, minute repeater and tourbillon chronograph, while the Edward Piguet has an arched rectangular case and also boasts remarkable technical feats. For its one hundred twenty-five year anniversary, the house lavished attention on communication and special events: the display of one hundred twenty-five historic models in the world's main capital cities and a charity auction at Christie's in New York were supported by the launch of celebratory pieces like an anniversary edition of the Star Wheel, a model from 1991 that displays the time through the interaction between three rotating disks (for the hours) and a special area where the minutes are marked out in an arch.

To celebrate the thirtieth anniversary of Royal Oak, the house capitalized on the synergy between AP Technologie and Renaud & Papi (a small manufacturer specialized in complicated movements and later taken over by Audemars Piguet), launching the Concept Royal Oak: featuring an avant-garde case made of alacrite 602, an exceptionally strong and resistant cobalt and chrome alloy used in the aviation industry, and a titanium bezel, the watch is waterproof up to five hundred meters. In the manual-winding mechanism, the tourbillon is flanked by a dymographe, which displays the mainspring's real-time torque. It also has a system for selecting crown functions using a button at four o'clock.

Left
Complete Calendar

Manual-winding watch with calendar, lunar phases and a white gold case, circa 1940.

Center
Complete Calendar

Manual-winding watch with complete calendar and a square yellow gold case, circa 1940.

Right
Complete Calendar

anual-winding watch with triple date calendar, lunar phases and a yellow gold case, circa 1930.

Perpetual Calendar

Self-winding watch with a perpetual calendar and yellow gold case, 1986.

Royal Oak is the foundation on which Audemars Piguet launched its City of Sails chronograph and Dual Time model, both dedicated to Alinghi, the Swiss yacht that won the 2003 America's Cup. This was by no means a chance move: Audemars Piguet is one of the sponsors of the legendary yacht, which brought the trophy back to Europe after an absence of 152 years. In the area of collaboration with famous figures in the celebrity star system, the Royal Oak Offshore T3, was dedicated to the actor and politician Arnold Schwarzenegger and the Montoya, which features elements in carbon fiber, inaugurated a partnership with Formula One drivers.

Royal Oak Offshore Alinghi Polaris

Rattrapante flyback chronograph with a self-winding movement and a steel case. Limited series of 2,000 pieces, 2005.

Concept Royal Oak

Manual-winding watch with tourbillon and dynamometer; case in alacrite 602. Limited series of 150 pieces, 2002. At left, the mechanism outside its case.

Royal Oak

Self-winding watch
with steel case
and bracele.

Royal Oak

Self-winding watch
with a rose gold case
and crocodile strap.

Royal Oak

Self-winding watch
with steel case
and bracelet, 1972.

Royal Oak Offshore Diver

Self-winding with a steel case, natural rubber strap and inner rotating ring with diving scale, waterproof to 300 meters.

Royal Oak Offshore Chrono

Self-winding in steel, waterproof to 100 meters, chronograph, date, small seconds and tachymetric scale. 42-millimeter case.

Jules Audemars Grande Complication

Self-winding with gold case and minute repeater, perpetual calendar with lunar phases and split seconds chronograp.

The Montoya was followed by limited series associated with the drivers Barrichello and Trulli, as well as a range of pieces commemorating world events. From the perspective of horology, we should note the watchmakers' remarkable achievements in the area of performance, including the first equation of time wristwatch with sunrise and sunset times and a perpetual calendar, the Audemars Piguet direct impulse escapement (2006) and the Jules Audemars Chronomètre of 2009, a high frequency chronometer (43,200 vibrations per hour) with a double balance spring and Audemars Piguet escapement. 2012 was the fortieth anniversary of Royal Oak, a model that has always been infused with an aura of excitement. One of the most sensational variations was the Royal Oak Offshore Carbon Concept Tourbillon (2008), the first watch with a forged carbon case and movement, a technological material in which the Le Brassus-based house has invested considerable research and development.

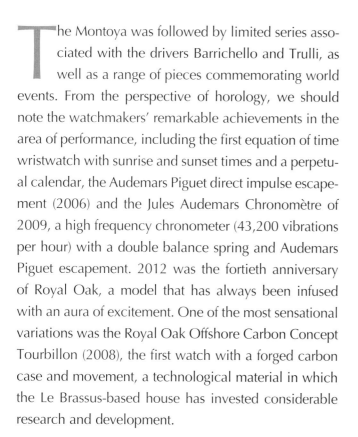

Royal Oak Chrono

Self-winding chronograph with a gold case, a tapisserie motif on the dial and luminescent and gold hour markers and hands.

Royal Oak Equation of Time

Steel self-winding watch with complete calendar, Leap Year indicator, lunar phases, equation of time and sunset and sunrise times for a location of one's choosing.

Royal Oak Extra-Thin

Steel with a 39-millimeter case and 3.05-millimeter high self-winding movement, 2012 production commemorating the original model designed by Gérald Genta in 1972.

Royal Oak Offshore Alinghi-Team

Chronograph with a regatta flyback function, made in a limited series of 1,300 pieces with a case and bezel in carbon and a vulcanized natural rubber strap.

Baume & Mercier

Always in search of perfect, harmonious proportions, Baume & Mercier is inspired by the classic shapes of horology. Its creations have also been influenced by current trends, combining essential lines with tradition and a sports spirit.

Left
Riviera
Watch with date and central seconds, twelve-sided case and link bracelet in steel and gold, quartz movement, circa 1990.

The Baume family, of French origin, began working in horology in the seventeenth century, after moving to Les Bois. In 1830, Baume Fréres was founded. In 1844, they opened a branch in London and, later, began exporting to Australia and New Zealand.

Riviera
Watch with twelve-sided case, Baumatic self-winding mechanical movement, 1975.

Catwalk

Cuff watch in steel with diamond decoration, quartz movement, circa 1990.

Tronosonic

Steel watch with central seconds, day and date, electric diapason movement, 1973.

the house's warhorse for the years to come. In 1988, Baume & Mercier, together with Piaget, passed to the Vendôme group (today, Richemont). Within Vendôme, the company was positioned as a brand offering classic timepieces with prestigious movements at a competitive price. During the 1990s, the manufacture focused on producing pieces of exceptional quality, both quartz and self-winding, introducing the Hampton, Classima, Catwalk and sporty Capeland. From then forward, Baume & Mercier has focused heavily on the Capeland models, its most sporty line, putting increasing emphasis on the dynamic expression of the latest trends.

Vice-Versa

Design watch in steel with large clasp and dial concealed beneath the strap. Right, a sketch of the watch.

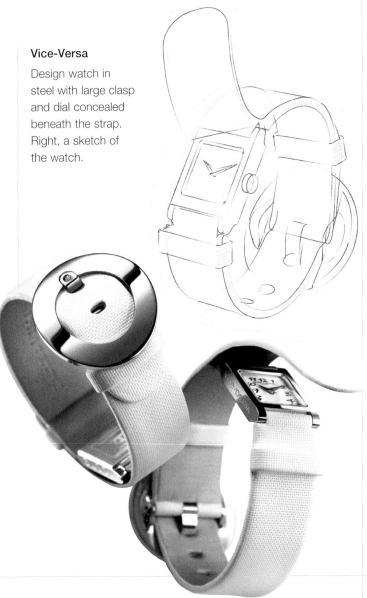

In 1912, William Baume met Paul Ceredicenko, a Parisian of Russian origin who was the head of Haas, a watch and jewelry company. Baume & Mercier was the result of this encounter (Ceredicenko having changed his last name to Mercier), with headquarters in Geneva. In 1937, William Baume left the company, and Constantin De Gorski, of Polish origin, took leadership. After World War II, Baume & Mercier won recognition for the Marquise, a lady's watch with a rigid bracelet that had no clasp. In 1958, De Gorski died and the company changed hands: Marc Beuchat became the new owner, but in 1965 the company changed hands again and was acquired by Piaget, one of the leading houses in haute horlogerie. In 1971, Baume & Mercier unveiled the Tronosonic line, which were watches with a diapason movement. Two years later, the Riviera line was introduced, with its characteristic twelve-sided case: this line would become

Vintage

Pocket watch with chain and wristwatch with alligator strap, both in steel and with, respectively, a manual-winding movement (with small seconds) and a self-winding movement (with central seconds and power reserve).

BR 01 Red Radar

Steel case with a PVD (Physical Vapor Deposition) finish, self-winding movement with disc display of hours, minutes and seconds.

BR Minuteur Tourbillon

Titanium case with a DLC (Diamond Like Carbon) finish, manual-winding movement with tourbillon and flyback minuteur.

A French company founded in 1992, it unveiled its first collection two years later. Its most successful models, the BR 01 Instrument and the BR 03 Instrument, are military in inspiration, drawing especially on the world of aviation.

Bell & Ross

The names of the founders—Bruno Belamich and Carlos A. Rosillo—gave origin to the company name Bell & Ross, a French house with production in Switzerland. Founded in the 1990s, it is distinguished for a highly personal collection with a strong character. Its first models, developed in collaboration with Sinn, a German firm specialized in military watches, bore the double name Bell & Ross – Sinn on the face. This was an important apprenticeship for Bell & Ross, from which it gained technical and design know-how, and led to the Hydromax, a timepiece distinctive for its watertightness up to 11,100 meters. Inside the case, one finds a hydraulic liquid that compensates for the pressure changes experienced during immersions at great depths. The experimental identity of Bell & Ross is based on its military production, and the company collaborates with a number of French assault units. In 1997, Chanel Horlogerie became a shareholder. In the third millennium, the company ended its partnership with Sinn (2002), starting up completely autonomous manufacturing activity based in La Chaux-de-Fonds. The Vintage 123, which has a distinctive round shape and results from a collaboration between Bell & Ross and the master watchmaker Vincent Calabrese, houses an intriguing mechanism with jumping hours and a power reserve indicator. This model was produced in many different variants, including a "three sphere" self-winding version and a chronograph, all with simple, instantly legible faces. But it was with the BR 01 Instrument, followed shortly after by the smaller-scale BR 03 Instrument, that the Parisian house established itself in terms of its creativity in wristwatch design. The design was directly inspired by cockpit command

Instrument BR 01–92
Self-winding watch with the brand's distinctive case shape, made in steel with a diameter of 46 millimeters. Synthetic canvas strap.

controls and the result was a watch with a square case, where the dimensions are masked by an effective formal equilibrium. In addition to the chronograph, the BR Instrument hosted movements with a dual time zone indicator, power reserve display and a tourbillon, becoming a popular model for customization and limited series, included the Radar line, where the hands have been replaced by rotating segments, and the Airborne, which has a dial dominated by a skull.

**Léman Tourbillon
Grande Date**

Self-winding watch
with tourbillon and
power reserve indicator;
rose gold case.

The company was founded in 1735, but Blancpain enjoyed its period of maximum splendor in the early 1980s. With a history of cutting-edge technology under its belt, its present-day profile is defined by uncompromising quality and the highest levels of artisan savoir-faire.

Blancpain

The horology adventure of Blancpain began in the town of Villeret, in the Swiss canton of Jura. It was there that Jean-Jacques Blancpain began producing timepiece movements, a tradition carried on by his son David-Louis, as was common practice for small businesses at the time. The turn came when Blancpain entered the competitive field of wristwatch design, an area that began increasing in popularity starting in 1920. An innovating spirit and the ability to develop cutting-edge technology led Blancpain to design the first mass-produced self-winding watch, the fruit of a partnership with the brilliant inventor John Harwood. In 1931, under license from the Parisian jeweler Léon Hatot, Blancpain dedicated its energy to the Rolls, a self-winding model with a special mechanism that used the oscillations of the movement inside the case to wind the barrel spring.

Air Command Concept 2000

Self-winding chronometer, with steel and natural rubber case, 2000.

Fifty Fathoms

Self-winding watch with steel case waterproof up to 50 fathoms (which equals 91.45 meters: 1 fathom = 1,829 m), 1953.

1950s advertisement for the Blancpain Fifty Fathoms.

Villeret 1984-2004

Self-winding watch with rose gold case;
limited series for the presentation
of the first Blancpain model,
with triple indication of calendar
and lunar phases, 2004.

In the 1950s, the house introduced the Fifty Fathoms watch, an intriguing waterproof model that accompanied Jacques-Yves Cousteau and his team while filming the documentary "The Silent World", which won the Palme d'Or at the 1956 Cannes Film Festival. During this same period, the Air Command was introduced, a chronograph for military use with an impressive size and equipped with flyback, a function that makes it possible to instantly return the elapsed seconds hand to zero and restart. The house remained committed to experimenting with solutions for robust, reliable timepieces with a predominantly masculine character. Its pieces sometimes bore the name "Rayville" on the dial, drawn from the company's new name, "Rayville SA Succ. de Blancpain".

After the successes of the 1950s, the company entered a rather long quiet period that ended in 1983 with the sensational entry of Jean-Claude Biver, a marketing man with extraordinary vision who saw potential in the Blancpain brand. Basing his communications strategy on the slogan, "Since 1735, there has never been a quartz Blancpain watch. And there never will be", Biver moved the manufacture's headquarters to Le Brassus, near the mechanism manufacturing firm that would become the exclusive Blancpain supplier, Frédéric Piguet. Those years saw the creation of masterpieces of rare elegance and an almost extreme technical character, demonstrating the boldness of the company's interpretation of the themes of classic horology. Complete calendar with lunar phases, rattrapante chronograph (which brought this complication back in fashion), perpetual calendar, minute repeater and tourbillon with an eight-day power reserve: a path of excellence that led to the unveiling, in 1991, of one of the most complicated watches in the world, which included each and every one of the horology specialties listed above: the 1735. Blancpain, now owned by the Swatch Group, has never lost is innovative character and dedication to constant research.

Harwood

The first self-winding
wristwatch, with a gold
case, circa 1920.

Rolls Ato

Self-winding watch
with a white gold case,
circa 1930.

The six master pieces

A special series of watches with platinum cases of the same diameter, distinguished for the use of mechanisms representing the best of watchmaking technology.
- Manual-winding ultra-thin
- Rattrapante chronograph
- Tourbillon with 8-day power reserve
- Complete calendar and lunar phases
- Perpetual calendar
- Minute repeater.

1735

Watch with self-winding mechanism made up of 740 components, with a platinum case, 1991. A masterpiece that includes a minute repeater, tourbillon, perpetual calendar, lunar phases and rattrapante chronograph.

The Blancpain atelier in Le Brassus, Switzerland.

A manufacture that inherited its style, elegance and ability to take on every complication with an innovating spirit from the father of modern horology, Abraham-Louis Breuget. The pieces produced by this house are united by certain signature features, like the "apple" watch hands, best known as "Breguet hands".

A portrait of
Abraham-Louis Breguet.

Classique Tourbillon
Wristwatch
with a gold case
and guilloché dial.

Breguet

The rotating tourbillon cage.

Upholding Abraham-Louis Breguet's exacting spiritual and intellectual legacy has always been the sole objective of his successors. Breguet was born in Neuchâtel in 1747 to a family of French origin that had immigrated to Switzerland upon Louis XIV's revocation of the Edict of Nantes, which forced Protestants to leave France, depriving them of all religious and civil liberties. Abraham-Louis Breguet, however, returned to France for an apprenticeship and to complete his training as a horologist, in part through interaction and exchange with the greatest experts in the field at the time, both French and English. Breguet learned a wealth of secrets from them about escapements and other structural components and his opening of a workshop on Quai de l'Horloge in Paris announced his achievement of full design mastery. His extraordinary creative gifts and unusual commercial approach made Abraham-Louis Breguet one of the eighteenth century's most fashionable horologists. Sovereigns and aristocrats found Breguet to be the ideal mind to suit their purposes, a master horologist capable of satisfying their desire to possess breathtaking timepieces for display on the most important occasions.

Tourbillon Chronograph

Manual-winding watch
with a yellow gold case
and a crocodile strap.

An image of the celebration at Versailles of the 200th anniversary of the invention of the tourbillon. At left, the mechanism outside its case.

Chronograph

Manual-winding watch
with a yellow gold
case, circa 1939.
Right, the mechanism.

Chronograph

Manual-winding watch
with a yellow gold
case, circa 1939.
Right, the mechanism.

Left
**Complete Calendar
Chronograph**

Manual-winding watch
with triple date indication
and a steel case, 1946.

Right
**Complete Calendar
Chronograph**

Manual-winding watch
with triple date indication
and a yellow gold case, 1964.

During that period, he produced some splendid por-
table models (pendulums
of unsurpassed technical and aesthetic
refinement; reliable and precise marine
chronometers), but it was with pocket watches that Breguet achieved the highest expression of his talent. Standing out among them is
the Marie Antoinette, a compendium of Breguet's
mechanical art that was created for the Queen of
France during the French Revolution and that, due to
the well-known chain of events that ended at the guil-
lotine by order of the people's tribunal, never came
into the possession of its legitimate owner. Misfortune
also struck this piece in later years: having been
donated to the Museum of Islamic Art in Jerusalem
by David Salomons, a great collector of Breguet timepieces, it was stolen in 1983. The Marie Antoinette
had a gold case with a rock crystal glass, dial and
cover and housed an extremely complex mechanism
with bridges, plates and some of the gears in rose
gold, screws in burnished steel and sapphire bearings.
The movement included the technical innovations
that had been Breguet's life's work: the self-winding
movement, interpreted differently than that introduced by Perrelet in the same period, the perpetual
calendar with equation of time, the thermometer, the
power reserve and the minute repeater (for chiming
the hours, quarter hours and minutes). Breguet worked
on the Marie Antoinette for more than twenty years,
during which time the world's most celebrated horologist continuously improved his own techniques.

We owe many other innovations to Breguet as well: the perpetual calendar for personal timepieces, a few escapement types, a spring with a special curve at the end, called the "Breguet spring", the "à tact" watch (which made it possible, using a special watch hand and tactile references on the case, to tell the time without taking the watch out of one's pocket, thus the avoiding the need to visibly check the time while conversing with someone, a practice already considered impolite at the time), the "pare-chute", a device designed to protect the balance pivots from shocks and, most important of all, the tourbillon, an invention still associated today with the name Breguet. The tourbillon is a mechanism designed to compensate, through a special structure called a "rotating cage", for timing errors caused by the effects of gravity on the balance spring. An extremely refined device and challenging to produce, it was designed at the end of the eighteenth century and patented in 1801. The list of Abraham-Louis Breguet's greatest admirers includes Napoleon Bonaparte, for whom he produced a few timepieces. Among them was a "pendulette officier" (also called a carriage clock), which was used by army officers during battles in the Napoleonic age. In his final years, Breguet tried to gather his horology experience in a highly detailed treatise, which was, however, left unfinished.

In 1823, the year of his death, leadership of the house passed to Antoine-Louis Breguet. Breguet's son maintained the company's relationship with the Royal French Navy, while production was primarily dedicated to complicated timepieces featuring major innovations, including a system for winding and setting the time without using a key, a solution that was quickly picked up by other houses, since at first the invention was not patented.

Perpetual Calendar

Manual-winding watch
with perpetual calendar
and a white gold case, 1934.
To the sides, two images
of the movement outside its case.
Below, the dedication
on the back of the watch.

SOUVENIR
DE JEAN DOLLFUS
A SON FRERE LOUIS
POUR SES 500 HEURES
DE VOL
DÉCEMBRE 1933

Minute Repeater
Manual-winding watch with a yellow gold case.

Quantième
Self-winding watch with complete calendar and a white gold case.

In 1833, Louis-Clément Breguet, Abraham-Louis's grandson, founded Breguet, Neveu et Compagnie and, among the pieces produced during that period one can even find a few wristwatches, however with characteristics far removed from the concept that would later take off in the early twentieth century. The company's customers remained the most important names in the European aristocracy, including Napoleon III of France, Queen Victoria of England and many leading figures of czarist Russia. Louis-Clément experimented with applying electricity to horology, opening up a technological direction dear to his son Antoine, who specialized in electricity and telecommunications (in the twentieth century, his great-grandson Louis Breguet would instead dedicate himself to aviation, working with an independent company).

The business was handed over to Edward Brown in 1870, an Englishman whose family would run the Breguet house for exactly one hundred years, shifting the manufacturing focus to wristwatches, particularly in the period between the First and Second World Wars. Breguet created

Héritage
Manual-winding watch with a non-circular yellow gold case, circa 1990.

Equation of Time
Self-winding watch with perpetual calendar, equation of time and a yellow gold case, circa 1990.

Quantième Perpétuel
Self-winding watch with perpetual calendar and a yellow gold case, circa 1990.

The modern Breguet manufacture, in Vallée de Joux.

Returning to the timeline of the company's history, 1970 marked the passage of Breguet from the Brown family to the Chaumet family, a Parisian dynasty of jewelers who opened a manufacturing atelier in Vallée de Joux, Switzerland in 1976. In 1987, the company was acquired by the Saudi Arabian group Investcorp, only to change hands again in 1999, when it was acquired by the Swatch Group. These were years when the focus on wristwatches was at its height, although a few refined pocket models were also produced. Among the wrist models, the preferred specialty was the tourbillon, paired with other complications and, of course, all of the special techniques developed by Abraham-Louis Breguet, reinterpreted for the needs of twentieth-century horology. In 2005, the La Tradition model made a splash at the Baselworld fair, featuring fascinating aesthetic solutions drawn from the house's history: the watch has a completely "visible" mechanism and represents the founder's inventions, presented in their original form, with the bridges and functional elements arranged just as Breguet would have positioned them two centuries earlier.

a range of splendid wristwatches, including models with round, square and "tonneau" cases, feminine versions with gold and diamonds, chronographs of rare beauty, calendars and tourbillons. The company then launched an important new chapter, supplying the air force with instruments and timepieces, presenting the Type XX, a wristwatch chronometer with a flyback function, which became one of the classics of sports horology. The production of "Breguet-style" watches continued with pieces with precious metal cases, the "carrure cannelé" (a fluted caseband), enamel or silver dials decorated with the guilloché pattern and completed with "apple" hands, universally known as "Breguet hands".

Classique

Self-winding watch with a yellow gold case and enamel dial.

La Tradition

Manual-winding watch with a yellow gold case.

Type XX

Manual-winding
chronograph with
flyback function and a
steel case, circa 1950.

Left
Lady

Manual-winding watch with
an Art Deco case in platinum
and diamonds, circa 1920.

Right
Reine de Naples

Self-winding watch with
power reserve, lunar phases
and a non-circular case
in white gold and diamonds.

Type XX

Manual-winding
chronograph with
flyback function, a steel
case and a dial with
three counters,
circa 1950.

Type XX Aéronavale

Self-winding chronograph
with flyback function
and a rose gold case,
circa 1990.

Classique Hora Mundi

Self-winding watch with instant-jump time-zone display of two time zones and display with the names of the twenty-four reference cities, red gold case and translucent lacquered dial depicting a choice of the Americas, Europe and Africa or Asia and Oceania, 2011.

1

Type XXII

Self-winding chronograph with flyback function and dual time zone, steel case with a graduated chapter ring.

2

Classique Grande Complication Tourbillon Messidor

Mechanical watch with aerial tourbillon enclosed between sapphire discs; rose gold case.

3

Marine Large Date

Self-winding watch with large date and 65-hour power reserve; steel case with natural rubber strap.

4

Marine Chronograph

Self-winding chronograph with 48-hour power reserve; gold case with natural rubber strap.

5

La Tradition

Mechanical watch with "old-fashioned" bridges and plates; white gold case.

6

Reine de Naples Cammea

Self-winding watch with white gold case, dial with cameo decoration carved out of a natural seashell, 2012.

1 2 3

4 5 6

Continuing along the path of tradition, but without ever losing sight of the avant-garde approach of the company's founder, the Double Tourbillon model was introduced in 2006, featuring two tourbillons visible through apertures on the dial. And it is a rotating dial, since the bridge that connects the centers of the cages of the two tourbillons ingeniously doubles as the hour hand. There is a Copernican revolution hosted inside the Classique model, round in shape and distinguished for its inclusion of all of the distinctive elements introduced by the Swiss house. In the area of sports watches and experimentation, one should note the developments of the Marine collection, featuring

watches usually made of precious materials and kept on the wrist with natural rubber straps, as well as the Type XXII, which has a silicon balance wheel and balance spring functioning at a frequency of 72,000 vibrations per hour. 2007 was an important year for the history of Breguet, with the sudden discovery of the original Marie Antoinette timepiece, followed one year later by the unveiling of the "contemporary" version, created on the impassioned initiative of Nicolas G. Hayek, the charismatic head of Breguet, who passed away in 2010. The timepiece was reconstructed using information gathered from archival documents and faithfully following Abraham-Louis Breguet's drawings.

Chronomat

Manual-winding
chronograph with a
steel case and a slide
rule chapter ring, 1942.

*A house famed for its precise, reliable chronographs, often selected for use
in commercial and military aviation. Breitling is dedicated to horological research
and development, with the aim of developing new technical and practical solutions
for its own models.*

Breitling

The history of Breitling began in 1884, when Léon Breitling opened a workshop in St. Imier in the Swiss Jura, specializing in manufacturing chronographs and precision timers for scientific and industrial use. In 1892, the manufacture moved to La Chaux-de-Fonds, the historic capital of horology, and built a factory on Rue Montbrillant, with the name "Léon G. Breitling S.A. Montbrillant Watch Manufactory". In 1915, it debuted the first wrist chronometer. The first technical development for this watch type dates to 1923, when the company patented its independent chronograph push-button which separated the stop/start functions from the crown (located at two o'clock). Three years later, it introduced a timer that measured time to one tenth of a second.

Willy Breitling, the founder's grandson, stepped in to take the helm of the business in the 1930s. 1934 saw the beginning of an important phase in the development of the house, with the introduction of a chronometer with two push-buttons: one at two o'clock for the stop/start functions, and another at four o'clock for resetting the various timers to zero. This was a fundamental innovation that anticipated the standard for modern wrist chronography.

Single-Button Chronograph
Manual-winding watch, with a chronograph push-button independent from the crown and a steel case, circa 1920.

Chronomatic
Self-winding chronometer, with a steel case, 1969.

Print ad from the 1930s celebrating the partnership between Breitling and the aviation world.

Navitimer

Manual-winding
chronograph with a
steel case and a slide
rule chapter ring for
aeronautical navigation,
circa 1950.

Cosmonaute

Manual-winding
chronograph, with a
steel case and dial
divided into twenty-four
hours, circa 1960.

**50th Anniversary
Navitimer**

Self-winding
chronograph,
with a white gold case;
limited series of
100 pieces, 2002.

Breitling became the supplier for a number of airline companies, including Royal Air Force, KLM, Air France and United Airlines. In 1942, the house, which also opened offices in Geneva, presented one of its manufacturing milestones: the Chronomat, a chronograph with a slide rule for performing complex mathematical calculations. This tool was especially useful in the aviation field: this model, in fact, let pilots calculate fuel consumption and average speed, allowing them to cross check the data provided by the flight instruments, which at the time were still only approximate. Ten years later, the Navitimer entered production, a watch that offered even more accurate calculations and which later evolved naturally into the Cosmonaute (1962). This model, worn by astronaut Scott Carpenter during his orbital flight on board the Aurora 7 spacecraft, featured a twenty-four-hour dial, rather than the usual twelve hours, to distinguish nighttime hours from day. In 1969, a joint project with Heuer-Leonidas and Hamilton-Büren resulted in the Caliber 11, a self-winding chronograph mechanism distinguished for having its push-buttons on the side opposite the crown.

In the 1970s, with the advent of quartz, production suffered a setback, but in 1979, Ernst Schneider, a pilot, watch manufacturer and microelectronics specialist, took over the Breitling brand and launched a new successful direction for the house which flanked the Grenchen facility with its historical production plants in La Chaux-de-Fonds. In 1984, the new generation Chronomat was unveiled, developed in collaboration with the Frecce Tricolori flight team, featuring a sturdy case and a rotating bezel with rider tabs. The chronograph movement was self-winding, and success was instant. The next year marked the market debut of the Aerospace, a technical instrument displaying both analogue and digital time, with an extremely light and shock resistant titanium case. This model opened the door to manufacturing technological watches like the Emergency (a multifunction timepiece with a miniaturized radio transmitter that functioned on the aircraft emergency radio frequency), the B-1 and the Colt Superocean, which could resist pressures up to 150 atmospheres. Breitling, which has held chronometer certification from the C.O.S.C. for all of its mechanisms since 2001, flanked its reissue of the classic Chronomat and Navitimer models with the Bentley Motors collection, developed for the prestigious British car manufacturer.

Emergency

Multifunction electronic quartz watch, with a titanium case and bracelet and an antenna operating on the 121.5 MHz international air distress frequency, circa 1990.

Chronomat

Self-winding chronograph with a steel case and bracelet, special series for the Frecce Tricolori flight team, 1984.

Transocean Unitime

Self-winding
chronograph in
steel with a waterproof
case, woven strap and
sapphire crystal on the
face and back, 2012.

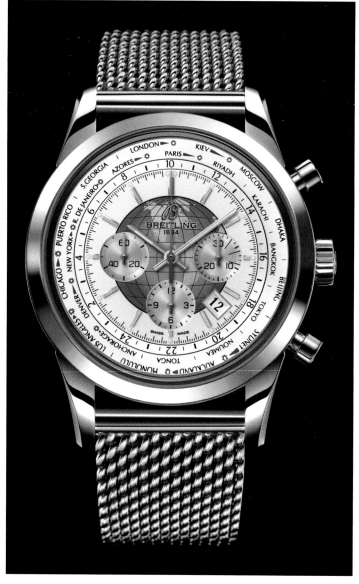

Navitimer World

Self-winding
chronograph with a
steel case, leather strap
and two-direction bezel
with a slide rule, 2005.

In order to meet the increasing demand for quality, understood as technical performance, mechanical excellence and a level of robustness able to take on any challenge, Breitling built Breitling Chronométrie in La Chaux-de-Fonds, a large-scale facility dedicated to the production and development of chronographs. In a building dominated by monumental works of art (Schneider is a passionate and savvy collector), movements are assembled with the aid of integrated software programs, which optimize time and precision, and automated stations alternate with watchmakers' workbenches. In 2009, the Caliber 01 was introduced, a synthesis of the full range of the manufacture's chronograph featuring a self-winding mechanism designed and produced in the La Chaux-de-Fonds ateliers, while standing out on the electronic front is the family of thermocompensated SuperQuartzTM movements, which are ten times more precise that traditional quartz calibers.

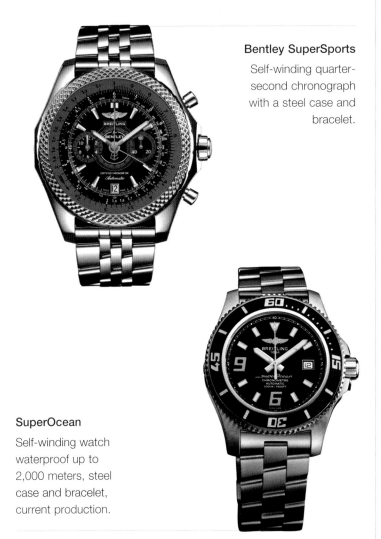

Bentley SuperSports

Self-winding quarter-second chronograph with a steel case and bracelet.

SuperOcean

Self-winding watch waterproof up to 2,000 meters, steel case and bracelet, current production.

Aerospace

Titanium watch, multifunction electronic quartz movement with mixed analog and digital display, 2007.

Chronomat 41

Self-winding chronograph with Breitling Caliber 01, steel case and bracelet, 2009.

One of the world's biggest names in jewelry, with headquarters in Rome, it produces elegant, distinctive watches that conquer connoisseurs with the evocative power of the Bulgari brand and the company's endless pursuit of aesthetic excellence and style.

Bulgari

Bulgari-Bulgari
Self-winding watch
with a yellow gold case,
circa 1980.

A path of excellence that began in another land: in 1884, Sotirio Bulgari, the heir of a dynasty of Greek silversmiths, opened his first shop on Via Sistina in Rome, which was followed in 1905 with the legendary storefront on Via Condotti. Horology became a part of the Bulgari world in the first half of the twentieth century, when the company began producing elegant watches that were as much timepieces as they were jewelry. But was not until the 1970s that the house began its unstoppable ascent, introducing the Bulgari-Bulgari in 1977 (designed by Gérald Genta), a model that displayed the house name on its smooth, flat bezel and would carry the company to the Olympus of haute horlogerie.

It was a sign that times were changing: the internationalization of the brand came with the opening of a horology department in Neuchâtel in the 1980s and single-brand boutiques in New York, London, Milan, Saint Moritz, Hong Kong, Singapore, Osaka and Tokyo, joining the "historical" shops in Rome, Paris, Geneva and Montecarlo as part of a strategy focused on the world's most important cities for business and pleasure.

*Varese, 1932:
Founder Sotirio
Bulgari vacationing
with his wife
and sons.*

Opposite
Bulgari-Bulgari

Electronic quartz watch
with a yellow gold case
and "Tubogas" bracelet,
circa 1990.

Quadrato

Electronic quartz watch with
a steel or yellow gold case,
circa 1990.

As for production, the company sealed an important partnership with Girard-Perregaux, which has supplied the mechanical movements for Bulgari watches since 1994. Standing out among the models from the 1990s are the quartz chronograph with a Bulgari-Bulgari case (later superseded by a self-winding version), the Quadrato and two grand complication models, the Tourbillon and the Minute Repeater. Next came the Sport collection, comprising a series of waterproof watches, like the Diagono Professional Scuba Chrono, a self-winding chronograph that was waterproof up to two hundred meters and complete with a chronometer certificate, screw crown and push-buttons, a single-direction bezel for immersion timing and an innovative natural rubber strap, fixed to the case with screws, with articulated, reinforced clasps. The increasing importance of Bulgari in terms of sales and its position in the luxury market was underlined by its listing on the Milan and London Stock Exchanges. Keeping its eye on expansion, the Bulgari Group acquired the brands Gérald Genta and

Aluminium Chrono

Self-winding chronograph
with an aluminum case
and a natural rubber
chapter ring and strap,
circa 1990.

Diagono Scuba Diving

Self-winding watch with
a steel case, waterproof
up to 2,000 meters,
2003.

Diagono Regatta

Self-winding chronograph
with functions designed
for sailing competitions
and a steel case.

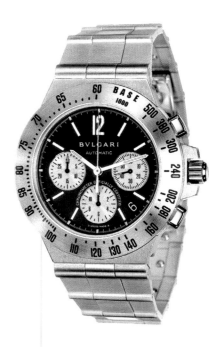

Diagono Tachymetric Chrono

Self-winding chronograph
with a steel case and bracelet
and a bezel engraved with the
tachymetric scale.

Daniel Roth in 2000. The Bulgari-Bulgari and Diagono lines were joined by Aluminium, a watch with a case made out of aluminum (an extremely light metal), a black PVD bezel and a natural rubber strap: another Bulgari success story. With jewelry being the sumptuous and elite soul of Bulgari, the house took care not neglect the female wearer and launched the B.zero1 line, a watch with a case resembling a Bulgari ring from the late 1990s, accompanied by a colorful strap.

In the sphere of professional timepieces, 2003 saw the launch of the Diagono Scuba Diving, a waterproof specialist watch with a valve for releasing helium and guaranteed watertightness up to 2,000 meters, followed by the Diagono Professional GMT Flyback, with a flyback chronograph (in French, "retour en vol") and GMT, and the Diagono Professional Regatta, with a chronograph for counting down the five minutes prior to the start of a regatta.

B.zero1

Electronic quartz watch with a steel case, available in a range of dials and straps.

With an ever-watchful eye on trends and new developments, Bulgari further diversified expanding its traditional offer of watches, jewelry, perfume and accessories to includes luxury hotels, opening the Bulgari Hotel in Milan in 2004, followed by a resort in Bali and the Bulgari Hotel in London. Bulgari has made important investments in horology, acquiring numerous companies specialized in high-end components in pursuit of its strategy for vertical integration. The fruit of these investments is the Caliber 303, a self-winding chronograph unveiled in 2007 that expresses the Roman house's renewed innovative spirit. The adoption of other exceptional mechanisms followed, while the company's creative achievements alternated between models for men, including the Sotirio Bulgari, launched for the house's 125th anniversary in 2009 and featuring a round case and triangular horns, and splendid creations for women, including the Serpenti collection, which reinvigorated the Bulgari Tubogas model, one of the Italian brand's great creative icons. 2011 was a year of epochal change for Bulgari, with its acquisition by the French luxury colossus LVMH, bringing with it the company's delisting from the Italian Stock Exchange.

Serpenti

Jewelry watch with a curved case, elastic yellow gold bracelet, diamond bezel and quartz movement.

Daniel Roth Carillon Tourbillon

Self-winding watch with three-hammer minute repeater, tourbillon, rose gold case and alligator strap.

Octo Maserati

Self-winding chronograph with a column wheel, jumping hours, chronograph timers, retrograde minutes and a steel case.

Diagono Calibro 303

Self-winding chronograph with a house-designed movement, 40-hour power reserve and a rose gold case with steel elements.

Diagono Ceramica

Self-winding chronograph with three timers, calendar, a rose gold case with ceramic elements and a natural rubber strap.

Bulova

The Bohemian Joseph Bulova and the American dream, the art of measuring time experienced as innovation and a knack for surprising the competition, like the Bulova Accutron with a tuning fork movement, the precursor of the electronic quartz watch.

The birth of Bulova is tied to the phenomenon of immigration to the United States in the late nineteenth century. In 1875, at just twenty-three years of age, Joseph Bulova, a young immigrant from Bohemia, opened a jewelry store in New York. The history of the brand was at first tied to the production of table clocks and pocket watches. In 1919, it presented its first collection of men's wristwatches, followed five years later by a line for women.

A Bulova print ad from the 1950s.

Accutron

Steel watch with an electronic tuning fork movement, circa 1960.

The American spirit of the house was emphasized by the founding of the Bulova Watch Company Inc. in 1923 and the strategic importance of the overseas market: in 1931, Bulova invested more than one million dollars in communications, and in the 1940s it sponsored radio programs and created a television commercial. Arde Bulova, the son of the founder, was especially dedicated to technical horology, producing military watches, flight instruments and reliable, robust mechanisms. But it was with the Accutron that Bulova became one of the leading companies in electronic horology. Using a tuning fork as a regulator, the Accutron promised and delivered significant levels of horological performance, making the model, which came in an infinity of variations, extremely sought-after by collectors. Acquired by the Loews Corporation in 1979, Bulova has always kept an eye on industry innovations, dedicating itself above all to quartz technology. In 2002, with the goal of commercial development on a global scale, Bulova opened a European office in Fribourg, Switzerland, pursuing a strategy focused on product internationalization and better handling of foreign markets.

Asymmetrical

Waterproof watch with a non-circular gold case and a Swiss movement with twenty-three rubies, circa 1960.

Hexagonal

Watch with a six-sided gold-plated case and a dial alternating hour markers and Arab numerals, circa 1950.

Crossed Horns

Watch with 14-carat gold case and distinctive for the unique design of its horns, circa 1950.

Ambassador

Gold chronometer produced in 2005 in a series of 130 pieces for Bulova's 130th anniversary.

Founded in Paris in 1847, the Cartier name has always been associated with the world of refined women's jewelry. In the horology sphere, the Santos model of 1904 launched more than a century of wristwatch history, marked by models distinctive for their unwavering taste and elegance.

Cartier

Santos

Manual-winding watch
with a gold case, variant
featuring a bezel attached
with studs, 1928.

The Cartier adventure began towards the middle of the nineteenth century when Louis-François Cartier acquired the jewelry shop of Adolphe Picard, in Paris. The inventiveness and talent of the young artisan were appreciated by the upper middle class, but also by royal figures, including Empress Eugenia, followed by many other representatives of prestigious families, who found their point of reference in the precious objects found in the Parisian atelier of Cartier. The brand's horological debut dates to 1853 and the first pocket models were sold to a clientele increasingly fascinated by the creativity of the high-end jeweler, as demonstrated by the watch-ring models produced starting in 1871. The family saga continued with the founder's son, Alfred Cartier, who took

The jeweler Louis Cartier, who masterfully led the house through its most extraordinary period of development, in a Belle Epoque drawing.

Santos

Manual-winding watch with a gold case, white dial with Roman numerals and a crown with a sapphire cabochon, circa 1920.

Opposite
Santos 100

Self-winding watch with a steel and gold case, produced for the 100th anniversary of the model's debut, 2004.

over management of the boutique three years later. In 1888, a collection of lady's wristwatches was introduced, which were in effect small pocket models attached to the wrist with gold bracelets. In 1898, Louis Cartier joined the business and, together with his brothers Pierre and Jacques, transformed Cartier from a simply successful company into a global luxury legend. Those were the years of the Belle Epoque, a historical period led by wealth, glamour and elegance: in 1899, Cartier moved its shop to 13 Rue de la Paix, a magnet for Parisian luxury, to take full advantage of the spirit of the times. The atelier became a point of reference for the French nobility and global aristocracy, and also the site of the Cartier archives, filled with leather-bound volumes that tell the story of the house's undertakings, reporting detailed information about the models sold and, most importantly, through the cataloging of the brand's designs and patents, tell the story of the evolution of the customs of contemporary society.

Santos Dumont

Mechanical manual-winding watch with a gold case.

Santos de Cartier

Self-winding watch with a steel case and bracelet.

Santos de Cartier

Quartz watch with a steel case and bracelet.

A flight pioneer in the Parisian skies, with the Tour Eiffel in the background, in an early twentieth-century photograph.

1904 was a fundamental year for the house: on request by the aviation pioneer Alberto Santos-Dumont, an extraordinarily wealthy Brazilian magnate and active member of Parisian society life, Louis Cartier created a wrist model. This was an innovation that many Swiss watch manufactures had been moving toward but, unlike the other experiments carried out at the time, this was the first true wristwatch in history: not merely an adaptation of the pocket watch, it was a completely redesigned object, where every element was conceived for a new way of reading the time that, in the span of just a few short decades, would supplant the pocket watch. The new model paired practicality with an elegant style, where the elements of the case—square-shaped in yellow gold with Roman numerals on the dial—and the strap were in perfect harmony. The eclectic Santos-Dumont could

thus check the time and his flight performance with the wristwatch designed for him by his friend Louis Cartier. After a period of experimentation, during which Cartier developed new shapes for its wrist models (the Tonneau was introduced in 1906), the Santos was made available on the market, with its name recorded for the first time in the house's registers in 1913, accompanied by the note 'Montre de forme carré dite Santos-Dumont' next to a drawing of the watch. The Santos became one of the Cartier trademarks, the catalyst of a collection for men and women that culminated, in 2004, the one-hundredth anniversary of its invention, with a reissue of the Santos Dumont in an ultra-thin gold version distinguished for its elegant slenderness, and the unveiling of the Santos 100, a self-winding model with a large case, with which Cartier rang in the new millennium. Another model linked to the genius of

Tank Jewelry Watch

Mechanical manual-winding watch with a platinum and diamond case, 1919.

Tank Française

Mechanical self-winding watch with a gold case, 1996.

Louis Cartier is the Tank. Also a watch with a non-circular case, picking up the square lines of the Santos, this model instead has two long bands at the sides that conjure up the tracks of World War I tanks, thus giving origin to the name of the model, the "Tank". In this case as well, the aesthetic achievement was a stroke of genius and the initial designs of 1917 were followed by the model's presentation on the market in 1919. The Tank initiated a dynasty of continuously updated wristwatch models, complemented by an endless variety of options for the case and bracelet, including the Tank Obus, with horns shaped like bullets, the Cintré, with an elongated case and a slightly curved back, the Asymétrique, with an asymmetric dial and case, and the Tank à Guichets, with jumping hours and a surface almost entirely covered with metal, displaying the hour and minutes in two small apertures.

Art Déco

Platinum, onyx, pearl and diamond watch with a bracelet complete with a safety chain, circa 1920.

The production of jewelry watches is one of Cartier's great traditions.

Tank Américaine

The Tank model in platinum, with a white gold crown and yellow gold clasp, made for the Prince of Nepal, 1943.

Tank Cintré

Mechanical watch with a platinum case and rose gold back, circa 1920.

Tank Heures Sautantes

Mechanical watch with a satin finish and digital display, made for the Maharaja of Patiala, 1928.

In addition to Cartier's two big stars, Santos and Tank, the house developed a wide range of timepieces, distinguished for their peerless creative brilliance. The metals utilized varied, with gold and platinum dominating, often embellished with rare precious stones, while the shapes were sophisticated and original. Models from the 1920s and 30s included the Cloche, with the numbers turned ninety degrees (the 12 coincides with the crown) and an option to use the watch as a bedside table clock, and the Tortue line, with sophisticated variations like the minute repeater or single-button chronograph, with the crown integrated into the chronograph command button. Cartier's timepieces were equipped with mechanisms of the highest level, manufactured by, among others, Edmond Jaeger (in accordance with an agreement signed in 1907, then renewed in 1919 until 1933), then Jaeger-LeCoultre following the merger between Jaeger and the Swiss LeCoultre. For export models, the models were usually stamped EWC (European Watch Company), a subsidiary of Cartier with offices in New York. Cartier dedicated itself without interruption to what one might call "alternative horology" for both its intended uses and the richness of its finishing touches, which drew on those of the jewelry world. Pendants and pins for ladies, with tiny mechanisms capable of marking the time, almost exclusively made for decorative use, were flanked by a healthy production of pocket watches in the most varied range of forms, the particularity of which often lay in the slenderness of the case and use of diamonds or hard stones.

Crash Watch

Watch with asymmetrical
gold and diamond
case, manual-winding
movement, 1992.

A n area in which
Cartier has always
demonstrated limit-
less creative capacity is that of
small clocks, producing exceptionally well-made table models. The
ornamental elements of the timepieces in
this category represent the height of richness and
imagination. Standing out among these masterpieces
is the "Mystery Clock", which entered production in
1913 and features hands that seem to float like magic
in the air. In reality, they are attached to serrated discs
set into motion by concealed gears and connected to
the mechanism in the base. The death of Louis Cartier
in 1942 marked the end of an age of extraordinary
successes. The Parisian house returned to its active
focus on development, put on hold by World War
II, with the introduction of new lines, including the
Crash Watch of 1967, with a crumpled case inspired
by Salvador Dalí's "melting clocks". In 1970s brought
with them an epochal change: in 1972, the founder's
last heir sold the company to a financial group, which
then became Vendôme Group, and later, Richemont
Group. The company's structure and distribution
model was given a new direction, with the goal of
achieving significant sales targets: in 1973, the "Les
Must de Cartier" collection was unveiled, a selection
of objects and watches focused on a younger, more
dynamic lifestyle, with special attention to providing
good value for money. The return to themes of the
past became a key productive strategy for the new
Cartier, starting with the re-issue of the Santos, offered
in steel and gold, in 1978.

Tonneau

Watch with
barrel-shaped
gold case and a
circular mechanical
movement, 1913.

Trasformista

Lady's gold watch
with a woven
bracelet and
concealed dial,
1942.

Cartier-London

Watch with a
lozenge-shaped
case and stylized
hour markers,
circa 1960.

Tortue

Platinum mechanical watch
with a turtle shell-shaped case,
circa 1920.

Single-Button

Gold mechanical watch with a
push-button coaxial with the
crown, 1928.

Pasha

Self-winding gold watch with a
protective grid on the dial and a
rotating graduated bezel, 1985.

A nother model representative of the house's new direction was the Pasha, unveiled in 1985 and inspired by a watch commissioned by the Pasha of Marrakesh in the 1930s. The Arab dignitary had requested a watertight model, which was then produced in the decade that followed and was distinguished for its large round case, glass protected by a metal grill and a crown protected by a cabochon cover fixed to the case with a tiny chain. The Pasha of 1985 preserved these features, making the metal ring optional and introducing a wide range of variants, followed in 2005 by a radical restyling of the model's aesthetic and mechanical components. The Tank Americaine and Tank Française similarly preserved the stylistic particularities of their namesake and Cartier icon, which was celebrated in 1997 for the 150th anniversary of the founding of the house. The presentation of a collection of intriguing histori-

cal watches, the stars of the celebratory auction "The Magical Art of Cartier", organized by Antiquorum and Etude Tajan and, later, distributed in a limited edition in Cartier boutiques, in fact included the "jump hour" Tank, with digital hours and minutes, the double-dial, double-crown Cintré, with two manual mechanical movements that could be set to two different times zones, the asymmetrical Tank with a "lozenge-shaped" case and the Tank with a pivoting basculante or reversible case. These were all extremely sophisticated models, expressive of a way of thinking about horology that showed full respect for tradition, as evidenced by the Collection Privée Cartier Paris, a line of complication models with high-end movements, gold dials and straps with the brand's distinctive folding clasp, universally known as the "deployant clasp", which was patented by Cartier in the early twentieth century.

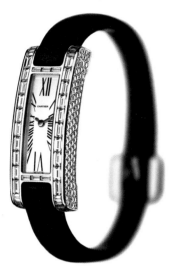

Jewelry watch

With a white gold and diamond case.

Top left, **Sabot** - center,
Tonneau, "lady's and gent's" pair -
bottom, **Sofa** and **Hypnose** -
right, **Casque.**

1

Santos 100

Steel self-winding watch celebrating the 100th anniversary of the model's debut.

2

Santos Dumont Skeleton

Skeleton watch with a mechanical movement, bridges shaped like Roman numeral hour markers and a white gold case.

3

Calibre de Cartier

Self-winding watch with three date calendar, small seconds and a steel case with a protected crown.

4

Tank Folle

Jewelry watch with an asymmetrical gold and diamond case and a mechanical manual-winding movement.

1

2

4

3

The creativity of the Parisian house has soared in designs for women, where luxury and refinement are paired with originality and transgression. This approach found perfect synthesis in the La Doña de Cartier, a watch dedicated to the Mexican actress María Félix who, in the 1970s, asked Cartier to create a necklace inspired by a stylized encounter between two crocodiles. The piece has a trapezoidal case and a bracelet with a rounded surface reminiscent of a crocodile's silhouette.

A completely different spirit inspired the Ballon Bleu of 2008, offered in versions for both men and women, featuring a sapphire-topped integrated crown built right into the case, creating a powerful and deliberate stylistic effect. As for Cartier's manufacturing savvy, the grand complication models in the Haute Horlogerie collection are flanked by the Calibre de Cartier, with a masculine case and the Calibre 1904 MC movement, which was developed in-house.

Ballon Blue de Cartier

Self-winding watch with a steel case and bracelet and a protected crown decorated with a cabochon.

Baignoire

Small electronic quartz model with a rose gold case, alligator strap and silver-plated dial.

Tank Américaine

Self-winding watch with a yellow gold case, alligator strap, silver-plated dial and guilloché decoration.

Chanel

It is a name that conjures up the world of high fashion and the elegance of simple lines, with an aura of singular fascination. In the collective imagination, Chanel represents the unpretentious luxury and strong personality of each of its products, inevitably inspired by Coco Chanel, the "Mademoiselle" who revolutionized twentieth-

Mademoiselle Coco Chanel in a famous photographic portrait with Place Vendôme in the background.

Just like the perfume Chanel N°5, the French haute couture house's horology is distinguished for its femininity and elegance. But it also has some surprises in store for men, like its high-tech ceramic J12 chronograph, an intriguing alternative in the sport watch realm.

J12

Self-winding watch with calendar, high-tech white ceramic case and diamond bezel.

Première

Electronic quartz watch with a steel case and a steel and leather bracelet, 1987.

Matelassée

Electronic quartz watch with a yellow gold case and bracelet.

century taste and remains today, with her incomparable style, the icon of reference for anyone contributing to reinforcing the Chanel "myth". In horology, this task was met by Jacques Helleu, who designed the Première model in 1987, featuring the Chanel logo on an octagonal dial, recalling the Parisian Place Vendôme, the site of the house's historic headquarters. It was an international success, as were other intriguing models, like the Mademoiselle of 1990, designed in open homage to the founder, with a perfectly square case embellished with gold and pearls or a distinctive "Chanel-style" leather chain. Or the Matelassée model, with a bracelet that picks up the quilted pattern of the brand's purses, and then the Chocolat, with a digital display and powerful aesthetic impact.

With the J12, unveiled in 2000, Chanel entered the field of men's timepieces, presenting a watch available in a range of options, like the "three spheres", chronograph and tourbillon, that wedded a sporting spirit, citing the world of cars and sailing in its details and colors, to a technological soul, with ceramic as the distinctive material used for its case and bracelet.

J12 Tourbillon

Manual-winding watch with ceramic and white gold tourbillon, original design by Jacques Helleu, limited series of twelve pieces, 2005.

Première

Two jewelry watches that represent the current evolution of one of the first Chanel timepieces, respectively produced in white gold, diamonds and pearls and steel, ceramic and diamonds.

J12 Rétrograde Mystérieuse

Ten exemplars in ceramic and white gold, with a retractable crown and a retrograde minute hand that travels from 10 to back to 20 minutes.

J12 Marine

Self-winding and waterproof up to 300 meters with a ceramic case, a natural rubber strap and an aperture for releasing water.

Première Tourbillon Volant

A unique model in white gold and diamonds created as a "bravura piece": the tourbillon cage has seventy-three components and a weight of 0.432 grams.

The model was an instant global success. The white and black ceramic versions were then joined by a titanium ceramic option called the Chromatic, with a hue alternating between the black and white of shot-silk reflections. The case diameters vary greatly to meet the needs of the international market, but the J12 has always preserved its pioneering spirit and timeless style. Sometimes adopting mechanics of considerable technical importance, like the J12 Calibre 3125, developed in collaboration with Audemars Piguet and distinctive for its gold and high-tech black ceramic rotor. Or the J12 Rétrograde Mystérieuse, a tourbillon with ten-day power reserve, digital minutes display and retrograde minutes, a prodigy transformed into a watch, thanks to the Chanel RMT-10 caliber, designed exclusively for Chanel by Renaud et Papi Manufacture. It was produced in a limited series of ten pieces, with a black ceramic case enhanced with white or rose gold.

Glamor and worldliness are the secrets to the success of Chopard, a house that in the 1980s adopted an approach to horology characterized by originality, sumptuousness, luxury and eccentric shapes, supported by an aggressive communications strategy and a constant presence on the wrists of VIPs.

Chopard

Mille Miglia

Chronograph with GMT function, self-winding mechanism and a steel case Limited series of 2,004 pieces, 2004.

The origins of Chopard date to 1860, when Louis-Ulysse Chopard opened a watchmaking workshop in Sonvillier, specializing in pocket chronometers and presenting his creations on long trips abroad, with a special focus on expansion in Eastern European markets. In the first years of the twentieth century, the company, enjoying constant growth, moved to Geneva and its production was distinguished for its catalog of traditional models.

The turn came in 1963, when Paul-André Chopard, the last heir of the founder and actively involved in the manufacture, decided to sell control of the company to the Scheufele family, first-class jewelers and owners of Eszeha, a jewelry company active in Pforzheim, Germany. In just a few short years, Karl Scheufele (assisted by his wife, Karin and, later their children Caroline and Karl-Friedrich as Vice Presidents) transformed Chopard into a house distinguished for the spirit and strong aesthetic impact of its designs for watches, jewelry and accessories. To meet the demand of an increasingly vast customer base, Chopard moved its offices to the new Meryin facility, in the industrial zone of Geneva. The distribution policy of the manufacture is intriguing, based as it is

Opposite
Mille Miglia

The back of the Chopard Mille Miglia, 2004 edition, celebrating the vintage car rally; steel case.

Print ad for the Mille Miglia race, 1935.

IX MILLE MIGLIA

14 APRILE 1935-XIII

EDE PROVINCIALE
BRESCIA

Chopard

(left margin)

Eszeha Chopard

Mechanical self-winding watch with a rose gold case. Right, women's manual-winding watch in rose gold. The two pieces were produced in a limited edition of one hundred pieces for the 100th anniversary of the foundation of Eszeha, the original company of the Scheufele family, 2004.

Selection of Chopard models from the 1969 catalog.

brating the prestigious annual Italian car race: a revival of a legendary competition in the 1950s, it is now a vintage car rally that winds through the roads between Brescia and Rome. The category of jewelry watches, which includes the Happy Diamonds collection as well as intriguing designs like the La Strada and the Ice Cube, is complemented by traditional models like the L.U.C. line (L.U.C. are the initials of the brand's founder), produced in the manufacturing atelier in Fleurier, located in the Val-de-Travers and the headquarters of the Chopard Manufacture. The masterpiece of this collection, with quality-stamped calibers and four barrels, for a longer power reserve, is the L.U.C. Quattro Tourbillon, a manual-winding watch with nine-day power reserve and a first-rate mechanism. Watches of rare beauty, chosen by the jet set and playing a starring role on the wrists of international celebrities, at the most exclusive events, including the Cannes Film Festival.

on just a few select dealers and a dense network of single-brand boutiques. The first Chopard shop opened in Geneva in 1986, followed by numerous other openings in the world's leading cities. In terms of production, the long list of the most successful models starts off in 1976 with Happy Diamonds, a collection for men and women that became one of the brand's best sellers, distinguished by the play of diamonds allowed to move freely on the dial. Four years later marked the arrival on the scene of the first Chopard sport watch, the St. Moritz, followed ten years after by what would become the brand's leading watch in this category, the Mille Miglia, with "three spheres" or a chronograph, cele-

L.U.C. Quattro Tourbillon

Manual-winding watch with tourbillon, nine-day power reserve and a rose gold case; limited series of one hundred pieces, paired with a further one hundred pieces in platinum, 2003.

Golden Diamonds

Watch with a white gold and diamond case.

Happy Sport

Watch with a steel case and bracelet, free-moving diamonds in a mother of pearl dial and a diamond bezel.

Haute Joaillerie

White gold and diamond baguette-style watches.

Chronoswiss

"The fascination of mechanisms" is the slogan of the house, which was founded in Munich by Gerd-Rudiger Lang in 1983. Those were years of change in horology, but Lang decide to buck the tide, defined by the unstoppable advance of quartz, instead choosing to use Swiss-made mechanical movements for his models.

Chronoscope
Self-winding
chronograph with
a "regulator" dial
and a steel case.

Founded in the early 1980s, Chronoswiss has carved out a place for itself among the top names in horology, thanks to its founder's firm commitment to producing exclusively mechanical watches that transmit the values of a long tradition.

Left
Kairos
Self-winding chronograph
with a steel and yellow
gold case and off-center
display of hours and
minutes, 1989.

The turn came in 1988, when Chronoswiss presented the Régulateur, a highly successful model with off-center hours on the dial, leaving pride of place for the central minute hand. The case for this model would become the house's trademark: a central, satin-finish cylindrical body topped by a screw-down knurled bezel and a transparent back, also encircled by a knurled ring, that reveals the finely-made movement. The model is completed by a large, knurled onion crown and curved horns, finished with two screws for attaching the strap. The Kairos was introduced in 1989, a mechanical chronograph with off-center hours and minutes. Chronoswiss ded-

icated itself to developing the Kairos and Régulateur lines, producing "time-only", self-winding chronograph and rattrapante hand variations. In 1994, the Grand Régulateur made its debut, driven by a Minerva pocket watch movement and designed so that it could be used as both a pocket watch and a wristwatch (the case has a special adapter). In the years that followed, the house introduced the Chronoscope, the first regulator chronograph and, for lovers of military-inspired watches, the large-scale (44 mm) Timemaster, with an optimally luminescent dial and over-sized crown. While for lovers of complications, the house unveiled the Régulateur Tourbillon and the Répétition à Quarts.

Timemaster Flyback
Self-winding chronograph with push-buttons and crown on the left-hand side of the case, in steel.

Tora
Self-winding chronograph with dual time zone and a steel case.

Timemaster
Manual-winding watch with an over-sized crown and a steel case, current production. Below, the Chronoswiss Timemaster Caliber C.672.

Corum has created some of the world's most original modern timepieces, thanks to its dynamic, avant-garde style, always aimed at developing a new way of conceiving the measurement of time, with some models that have become a contemporary symbol of fun, colorful horology.

Corum

Corum was founded in 1955 by Gaston Ries and his nephew René Banwart, who had worked at Patek Philippe and Omega: the first collections, presented under the name Corum (from the Latin "quorum"), attracted substantial interest at the 1956 Basel Fair. In the 1960s, René's son, Jean-René Banwart, also joined the company management. Corum's rise came with a model that combined high-impact aesthetics and originality: the Coin watch, created in 1964, had a case made out of an authentic gold coin, cut so that one side served as the watch dial and the other as the back. The Americans were enamored with this extraordinary object, which was later made using a twenty-dollar coin (the so-called "Double Eagle"), winning the house global success.

Coin Watch

Two versions of the watch, made with real gold coins, circa 1960.

Another historic Corum collection is the Admiral's Cup: linked to the world of sailing and especially to the competition from which its name derives, the line was launched in 1960 with a square-shaped, waterproof model with the outline of a mid-race sailboat on the back. The models from the 1980s testify to deep changes in the Admiral's Cup design, with the case becoming twelve-sided and the dial displaying the flags of the international code of signals.

Golden Bridge

The two original versions from the 1980s, with a baguette movement made by Vincent Calabrese.

Opposite
Golden Bridge

Manual-winding watch with a rose gold case and sapphire crystal, baguette movement with a crown at six o'clock; special series of fifty pieces made in 2005 for Corum's fiftieth anniversary.

Meteorite

Gold chronograph with a dial carved out of a real meteorite, circa 1980.

To make a brand grow that was already well-known for its avant-garde approach, Wunderman focused on wedding tradition and imagination. Production was organized into three distinct watch lines, with innovative collections mixed with reissues of models from the past distinguished for their strong stylistic and technical impact, as well as the splendid watch-cum-jewelry models that had been part of the Corum brand since its beginnings. The watch most symbolic of Corum's recent history is unquestionably the Bubble. Introduced in the year 2000, it returned the name of the house back to the hit parade of connoisseurs' most sought-after brands. It features a large

Bubble
Watch with a steel case and blatantly curved sapphire crystal, circa 2000.

Privateer
Bubble series variant, special edition of 250 steel pieces.

In 1980, the brand launched the Golden Bridge. This watch, developed with a patented design by Vincent Calabrese, had linear gear trains and a gold bridge. The whole was enclosed within a case that associated the gold structure of the mechanism and the case itself with Baccarat crystal. The 1990s saw the creation of exceptional models that further added to the house's fame, but it was in the year 2000, with the sale of the company to Severin Wunderman, that Corum began a new season filled with success.

(up to 45 mm in diameter) steel or gold case and, unique of its kind, a cupola-shaped sapphire crystal, which makes almost all of the models two centimeters thick. Another characteristic element of the design is its dial, which is always brightly colored and often imaginatively enameled and featuring characters often inspired by the world of comics. Standing out among the variations are the Jolly Roger, with a pirate skull and bone-shaped hands, the "diabolic" Lucifer, the Casino, with a dial mimicking a roulette wheel, and the Bubble, commemorating the "Flying Tigers" squadron, famed for its World War II victories, with dials reproducing the colorful designs of fighter planes.

Admiral's Cup Tides

Self-winding steel chronometer with a device for measuring the tides in relation to the phases of the moon.

Admiral's Cup Regatta

Self-winding steel chronograph, self-winding movement, certified chronometer, hour markers shaped like the flags of the international code of signals.

Daniel Roth

Tourbillon

Manual-winding watch with tourbillon, calendar, power reserve indicator and a non-circular platinum case, circa 1990 Below, the secondary dial of the Daniel Roth Tourbillon, visible on the back of the watch.

A passion for one of the greatest figures in the world of watches, Abraham-Louis Breguet, guided Daniel Roth in the two most important stages of his professional life. It is in fact to Roth that we owe renewed interest in timepieces by the modern Breguet Manufacture (now owned by the Swatch Group) on the cusp of the 1980s, thanks to a brilliant creative vision that contributed to the brand's global revival.

Inspired by the genius of Abraham-Louis Breguet, Daniel Roth has developed a series of pieces under his own name that, starting with the Tourbillon, revisit the grand complications of horology, committed to the most refined mechanisms and techniques.

Quantième Perpétuel Squelette

Self-winding watch with perpetual calendar, skeleton movement and a rose gold case.

Skeleton Chronograph

Manual-winding watch with a skeletonized movement and a yellow gold case, circa 1990.

Tourbillon Rétro Date

Self-winding watch with tourbillon, calendar with a retrograde hand and a rose gold case.

After this fruitful collaboration, Roth decided to open his own atelier in Le Sentier, in the Vallée de Joux, in 1989. One year later, he presented the Tourbillon, a piece that fascinates for its mechanical beauty and stylistic sophistication as well as for its reinterpretation of old artisan traditions, underlined by the case, which has an unusual semi-elliptical shape, a strong design later extended to other models, including women's watches. This technical achievement was followed by the Minute Repeater and the production of two- and three-timer chronographs, manual-winding or self-winding, perpetual calendars and models with retrograde indicators. Among the most striking aesthetic details in Daniel Roth timepieces are the dials, which are distinguished by either a guilloché pattern or a series of slender lines, interrupted by silver elements hosting the hour circle. One should also note the house's double dial, especially in the Tourbillon and Perpetual Calendar, which allows the displayed indications to be harmoniously arranged, with auxiliary information on the second dial on the back, carefully protected by a sapphire crystal. In the year 2000, the Daniel Roth brand was acquired by Bulgari, and production, always oriented towards the top range, was slightly restyled, maintaining, however, the high quality of its mechanisms.

De Bethune

DB15

Perpetual calendar with three-dimensional indication of the lunar phases and a gold case.

De Bethune, a company with a strong artisan identity, was founded in 2002 in La Chaux L'Auberson, Swiss Jura, by David Zanetta, an expert vintage watch dealer who upon creating this house has dedicated himself to producing models in the old style. Large cases with ogival horns, mechanisms refined with obsessive care and distinguished for their new technical solutions and gold dials for uncompromising quality.

Unwavering quality, full respect for old masters, the highest attention to new developments and products that are at once classic and the fruit of avant-garde research. De Bethune's genius lies in creating pieces with modern content and time-honored style.

3D Moon

Manual-winding movement for the DB15, with power reserve of more than four days, fully wound.

Only a few pieces are produced each year, often developed on request by wealthy customers and passionate collectors and in accordance with special criteria. One of the house's most intriguing models is the Single-Button Chronograph, with a chronograph hand and 45-minute chronograph counter, but without other accessory indications, for an ultra-thin mechanism of exceptional value (the case measures 8 mm thick). The principle of maximum legibility is enhanced by the stylistic rigor of the dials, where the placement of the name of the brand always keeps a low profile in favor of the more effective display of information, like in the Perpetual Calendar, with a dial featuring a stunning blued steel and platinum sphere illustrating the lunar phases.

Single-Button Chronograph

Manual-winding chronograph with 45-minute chronograph counter and a rose gold case.

In the area of mechanisms, in 2004, De Bethune introduced a caliber designed and produced entirely within the manufacture, boasting innovative technical solutions and a newly-conceived balance wheel with a titanium center and platinum outside weights, creating an ideal inertia-mass ratio that improves performance. It is accompanied by a spring with a special terminal curve, patented by De Bethune. The brand's excellence in technical and aesthetic research was recognized in 2011 with the Aiguille d'or, a prize awarded to the De Bethune DB28 at the Grand Prix d'Horlogerie in Geneva.

DBS

Watch with three-dimensional indication of lunar phases, a platinum case and manual-winding mechanism visible on the side of the dial.

Balance Wheel

Technical drawing of the innovative regulator developed by De Bethune: in titanium and platinum with a customized wheel.

de Grisogono

Occhio Ripetizione Minuti

Watch with a rose gold case
and diaphragm dial.
Below, the opening of the
dial diaphragm.

De Grisogono, first a jewelry house that later added watch-making to its production, distinguished for creativity and strong technical and aesthetic impact, was only founded in 1993, but draws on the long experience of Fawaz Gruosi, who brought sensitivity, beauty and new ideas to the luxury sector. With de Grisogono, Gruosi became free to

A creator of overtly displayed luxury, with a strong stylistic impact and an imaginative approach that downplays the richness of dazzlingly beautiful gems. This is de Grisogono, with Fawaz Gruosi in the role of its eclectic director.

dedicate himself fully to what he likes best, giving form to his personal way of "feeling" jewelry and watches, with a focus on innovating, exciting and transforming the wearable object into an experience that is above all sensual in nature.

De Grisogono made its debut in the world of horology in the year 2000 with Instrumento N° Uno, the first in a series of models often embellished with gems, including the black diamond, a stone revived by Gruosi and made into the emblem of his designs. The first model, with a non-circular case and

a self-winding movement with GMT and big date, was followed by Instrumento Doppio, with chronograph, second time zone, reversible case and indications on both dials. In 2005, after further variations on the Instrumento model and a few lines of jewelry watches for women, came the Occhio Ripetizione Minuti, an extremely precious model: in addition to the minute repeater (which sounds the hours, quarter hours and minutes on command), it has a diaphragm on the dial which opens when the repeater is triggered. This innovation was unique for its inventiveness, eccentricity and desire to amaze: in perfect de Grisogno style.

Instrumento N° Uno

Watch with dual time zone and big date, self-winding with a white gold and diamond case and black and white dial.

Instrumento Tondo

Watch with power reserve and analog calendar, self-winding with a white gold case.

Instrumento Doppio

Chronograph with dual time zone and big date, self-winding with a rose gold case and a double dial.

Ebel

Sport Classic
Electronic quartz watch
with a steel and gold case
and bracelet, 1977.

The history of Ebel is a romantic one. Its name is expresses the personal and professional intimacy of its husband-and-wife founders, combining the initials of Eugène Blum and the first initial of Alice Blum's maiden name, Lévy, linked by the conjunction "e" (meaning "and"): "E.B. e L.", or Ebel. The company was founded in 1911 in La Chaux-de-Fonds, and in addition to supplying fine movements and cases to other horology companies, Ebel also produced its own timepieces. Some of the brand's models

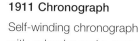

1911 Chronograph
Self-winding chronograph
with calendar and a rose
gold case, circa 1990.

Style, elegance and design are the defining characteristics of Ebel. Starting with its headquarters, located in the Villa Turque in La Chaux-de-Fonds since 1986, a structure designed by the Swiss architect Charles Edouard Jeanneret, better known by his pseudonym, Le Corbusier.

Tarawa

Self-winding watch with a steel case.

for women were especially captivating, embellished with diamonds and stones and distinguished for their refined, elegant lines. The manufacture continued to advance its technical research, and set itself apart for its adoption, starting in 1935 and well ahead of its competitors, of quality and precision control tools for its own production chain.

The turn came in the 1970s, with the entry of Pierre-Alain Blum, who introduced fundamental stylistic innovations to the brand. Under his leadership, the company completely overhauled its strategy, inspired by modern, sophisticated lines as emphasized by the company slogan, "Ebel, the Architects of Time". In the 1980s, the house achieved definitive success, in part through its special tie to the world of architecture. The launch of the Sport Classic collection, with five screws around the dial and a bracelet with a wave motif, was followed by the Beluga, 1911, Discovery, Lichine and Tarawa (with a curiously wavy case) lines. The house changed hands numerous times starting in the 1990s: in 1996, the Blum family sold the company to Investcorp, after which it was acquired by LVMH in 1999 and finally, five years later, by the Movado Group.

Extra-fort, Tazio Nuvolari and Chrono 4 are the best-known and most appreciated models in the wide range of wrist chronographs that have distinguished the history of Eberhard, a Swiss manufacture specialized in the mechanical measurement of time since 1887.

Eberhard & Co.

The central headquarters of Eberhard & Co. in La Chaux-de-Fonds, in an early twentieth-century photograph.

Founded in 1887 by Georges-Emile Eberhard in La Chaux-de-Fonds, the company special-ized from the beginning in producing chronographs. The first designs were pocket models, and the first wrist model was unveiled in 1919. This model made a major splash during that exciting period of pioneer-ing horology: manual-winding and single-button (the start, stop and reset functions were managed by a sin-gle button at two o'clock), it also featured a dial with a tachymetric scale, a hinged case back and straight horns soldered to the case for holding the strap, as was usual for chronographs at that time, which had been developed rather primitively from late nine-teenth-century pocket models. Continuous refinement allowed Eberhard & Co. to expand its collection in the 1930s to include self-winding watches and increas-ingly sophisticated chronographs, as demonstrated by its two-button chronographs and the inclusion of an hour counter on its wrist chronographs (1938). Those

Chronograph

Single-Button watch with a chronograph button at two o'clock, manual-winding with a yellow gold case, 1919.

Chronograph

Manual-winding watch with a steel case and a pink dial with a tachymetric and telemetry scale, circa 1930.

Chronograph

Manual-winding watch with a yellow gold case and black dial with a tachymetric and telemetry scale, circa 1930.

Opposite
Chronograph

Two-Button watch, manual-winding with a steel case, circa 1940.

Extra-fort

Double manual-winding chronograph with a yellow gold case and three-timer dial, 1950.

were the years during which the manufacture partnered with the Italian Royal Navy for the supply of officers' watches. A recognition of preeminence confirmed by the production of a rattrapante chronograph, dated 1939, with the button dedicated to this function co-axial with the crown and a case diameter well beyond the standard. The 1950s saw the debut of the Extra-fort, a two-button chronograph with a classic design, two timers and Dauphine hands, distinguished by the singular function of the button at four o'clock: its sliding push-button (as opposed to a pressure operated push-button) made it so that the chronograph hand could be stopped and restarted while keeping track of how much time had passed.

Tazio Nuvolari
Vanderbilt Cup

Vanderbilt Cup self-winding chronograph with a steel case and double snap-open case back.

Left
Traversetolo

Manual-winding watch with a large steel case and a black and white dial, circa 1996.

Tazio Nuvolari

Self-winding chronograph with a yellow gold case, black dial and perlage decoration on the bezel.

The company's steady development suffered a sudden interruption in 1962, when the founder's grandchild died in a tragic accident. The Eberhard family decided to entrust management of the house outside the family and the company continued its activity balancing respect for tradition with new developments, as expressed in its Caliber Beta 21 quartz model (1967) and adoption of mechanisms that functioned at 36,000 vibrations per hour. After a quiet period, Eberhard & Co. returned to the fore in the 1980s with its sponsorship of the Italian sailing team for the 1983 America's Cup and, in 1986, the acrobatic flight team Frecce Tricolori, and with the watches designed in celebration of these partnerships. In celebration of its 100th anniversary, the company debuted the Navymaster (1987), which was followed by the Mareoscope, with a tide indicator and, in 1992, the Tazio Nuvolari, a self-winding chronograph that was met with great success and featured timers at twelve o'clock and six o'clock, the turtle good luck charm of the Mantua pilot on the dial and a "rosette" bezel, a motif similar to perlage decoration and reminiscent of the dashboards of vintage cars. The Traversetolo, with a 43-mm case, and the 8 Jours, with an eight-day power reserve, together opened the path to mechanical watches with extended power reserves, accompanied by a major innovation in 2001, the Chrono 4: this revolutionary chronograph radically changed the positioning of the four timers (accompanying the chronograph timers with a twenty-four hour indicator), aligning them horizontally, while for the Temerario of 2005 they were vertically aligned.

Chrono 4 Temerario

Mechanical chronograph, self-winding with a "tonneau" steel case and unique vertically arranged timers.

A passion for sport watches was expressed in the Scafodat model of 2006, a powerful design with a watertight case engineered to withstand extreme depths, while the Gilda women's watch collection of 2010 expressed the brand's feminine side, featuring elliptical lines for the case, lending softness to the whole and heightening precious details emphasized by the diamonds and mother of pearl decorating the dials.

The first years of the third millennium have been dedicated to the celebration of important anniversaries for Eberhard & Co., with 2007 marking 120 years for its rich collection of chronographs and 2011 being the ten-year anniversary of the Chrono 4: to acknowledge this milestone, the dials of the Chrono 4 Géant Titane and the Chrono 4 Grande Taille have a large red Roman numeral "X" to mark the tenth hour. The next year, the Extra-fort conjured up the look of the past in honor of the Swiss house's 125th anniversary.

Gilda

Quartz watch with an elliptical steel case, mother of pearl dial with large Roman numerals and an alligator strap, 2010.

8 Jours Grande Taille

Manual-winding watch with eight-day power reserve indication on the white or black dial and a window on the back protected by sapphire glass and revealing the barrel bridge, 2008.

Tazio Nuvolari Data

Self-winding chronograph with two timers, a steel case, alligator strap, black dial with a "perlée" design, luminescent indications and red details.

Extra-fort

Self-winding chronograph with two timers, a steel case with a transparent back and alligator strap, 2009.

Chrono 4 Grande Taille

Self-winding chronograph with four horizontally arranged timers for small seconds, twenty-four hours and chronograph hours and minutes; steel case, 2008.

Chrono 4 Géant

Self-winding chronograph with four horizontally arranged timers for small seconds, twenty-four hours and chronograph hours and minutes; large case (46 mm diameter), 2010.

Eterna

Left
1935
Manual-winding watch
with a rectangular
steel or gold case,
1935.

F ounded in 1856 by Josef Girard
and Urs Schild in Grenchen,
Eterna was at first dedicated to
producing "ébauches", incomplete
mechanisms supplied to other houses
who would then complete and mount
them. The first Eterna branded pocket
watch dates to 1876. In the years that
followed, house production was clearly divided between Eterna, the brand
that produced complete timepieces,
and ETA, which worked exclusively on
movements.

Eterna-Matic

Self-winding watch,
mechanism with rotor
mounted on ball bearings and
a steel case, circa 1950
Below, the back of the case.

*Precision and absolute reliability are the
strong points of Eterna, a historic Swiss
brand whose name is linked to one of the most
incredible feats in modern history: explorer
Thor Heyerdahl's transoceanic voyage
on board a raft.*

Porsche Design

Self-winding chronograph
with a titanium case and
a natural rubber strap
in a limited series of
1,911 pieces.

Porsche Design Indicator

Self-winding chronograph
with a titanium case, natural
rubber strap and digital
indication of chronograph hours
and minutes, in a limited series
of 75 pieces.

Kontiki

Self-winding watch
with analog calendar
and a steel case.

In 1914, the house debuted the first wristwatch with an alarm, patented in 1908, a technological achievement of major importance. The brand's first self-winding movement instead dates to 1939. Three years later, Eterna unveiled a chronograph with a pulse meter that displayed the wearer's heart rate on the dial, while at the end of the 1940s the house launched a self-winding model with a rotor mounted on ball bearings, the famous Eterna-Matic, a technical development of such importance that it became part of the brand's denomination. The logo on the dial also reflected this innovation, featuring five spheres arranged in their distinctive arrangement inside the bearing. But it was in 1947 that Eterna joined the ranks of watch manufacturers that had played a part in legendary feats: the Norwegian ethnologist and adventurer Thor Heyerdahl wanted to demonstrate that it would have been possible to travel by sea from Peru to Polynesia in ancient times. With a raft made of balsa wood (named the Kon-Tiki), Heyerdahl crossed the Pacific Ocean to prove his theories: and he was accompanied on this adventure by an Eterna watch. The next year saw the debut of the Kontiki, a model designed in commemoration of that event and the first in what would become the brand's most successful line. The Kontiki 20, waterproof up to 200 meters, was followed by the world's smallest self-winding caliber and the Museum, with a quartz movement and overall thickness of 0.98 mm. In the 1990s, Eterna reissued a series of models from its past and, after Ferdinard Porsche's acquisition of the company, focused part of its production on creating Porsche Design watches, with a distinctively sporty style.

F.P. Journe

Left
Octa Chronographe
Self-winding chronograph with a platinum case and gold dial; current production.

François-Paul Journe approaches the world of watchmaking with great creativity, drawing deep inspiration from the past and re-reading the lines traced by great masters. Born in Marseilles, Journe received his professional training in Paris and Geneva, then opening his own business in 1999. Each year, he produces just a few pieces, which are well-known and admired by connoisseurs

A manufacture that came to the fore of luxury watchmaking in the 1990s, transforming the lyrical and technically exemplary intuitions of François-Paul Journe into watches. Journe is a brilliant watchmaker, able to confer a time-honored style to mechanisms, cases and dials.

Tourbillon Souverain
Manual-winding tourbillon with a platinum case and a gold dial.

of esoteric horology, for whom F.P. Journe-Invenit et Fecit (a Latin phrase borrowed from the horologists of the past, who used it to sign their mechanisms: for Journe, it highlights the design and conceptual path that leads to the organic development of each piece) is a point of arrival.

François-Paul Journe with a watchmaker's lens and tweezers, in his atelier in Geneva.

His watches are distinguished for their perfect mixture of styles, combining Baroque and minimalist elements: the silver guilloché dials are attached to a gold base with tiny screws and some special series are distinguished for their ruthenium treatment, which lends a special gray coloration to the base of the dial and the mechanism. The movements are exceptionally fine. They are always mechanical and, in recent years, produced with gold bridges and plates.

Octa Lune

Watch with power reserve indicator, complete calendar and lunar phases, self-winding with a platinum case and gold dial.

Chronomètre a Résonance

Manual-winding watch with a double mechanism and dial, a platinum case and a gold dial.

The most precious Journe collection is unquestionably the Souvrain line, which includes such models as the Tourbillon and the Chronomètre à Résonance, a watch that uses two balances and the resonance phenomenon to ensure better chronometric precision. The Octa series, instead, has a single "frame" for all of its models (in the sense that the plate and certain elements are common to all), including the Rèserve de Marche, the Chronographe and the Calendrier. As for the cases, here we have an inversion with respect to traditional horology: they are almost exclusively produced in platinum and gold, with steel reserved for the most expensive unique pieces and aluminum used for the Sport collection.

Octa Calendrier

Self-winding annual calendar with a platinum case and a gold dial.

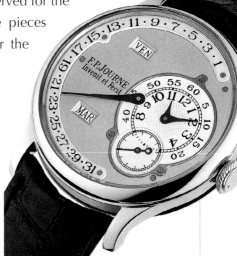

F.P. Journe

113

Franck Muller

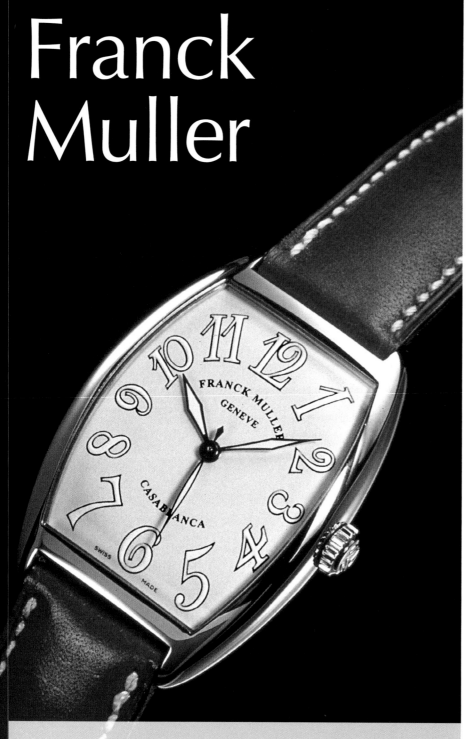

Imagination and technique, color and artisan tradition: Franck Muller represents the values of Swiss horology reinterpreted with a contemporary spirit and a modern vision of time.

Left
Casablanca
Self-winding watch with a Cintrée Curvex steel case, circa 1990.

The story of Franck Muller is tied to his skill in transforming his own artisan talent over the years into an organized enterprise with a strong productive capacity. Born in 1958, Muller, upon completing his training at the École d'Horlogerie de Genève, decided to dedicate himself to restoration, an art that gave him an opportunity to learn the most refined techniques and get to know the world of collecting. He later became a consultant at auction houses and major foundations.

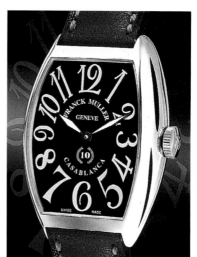

Casablanca 10th Anniversary
Self-winding watch with a Cintrée Curvex steel case from a series celebrating the tenth anniversary of Casablanca, 2004.

Crazy Hours Tourbillon

Watch with tourbillon, jumping hours and a platinum case, 2004.

Technical drawing of the Tourbillon Revolution 2.

Double Mystery

Self-winding watch with a platinum rotor, white gold and diamond case, diamond and sapphire dial and triangular hour and minute indicators.

Vegas Diamonds

Self-winding watch with a white gold and diamond case, Vegas function with a rotating roulette wheel in the center and a fixed time indicator.

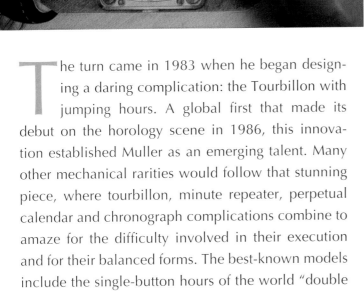

The turn came in 1983 when he began designing a daring complication: the Tourbillon with jumping hours. A global first that made its debut on the horology scene in 1986, this innovation established Muller as an emerging talent. Many other mechanical rarities would follow that stunning piece, where tourbillon, minute repeater, perpetual calendar and chronograph complications combine to amaze for the difficulty involved in their execution and for their balanced forms. The best-known models include the single-button hours of the world "double face" chronograph (the indications are on both dials, with the secondary dial visible on the back) and the Casablanca, one of the house's best-selling models, which celebrates the case design most typical of Franck Muller's production, the Cintrée Curvex, with an elongated "tonneau" shape and deeply curved back, making it optimally wearable on the wrist.

Success spurred Muller to realize one of his greatest dreams, inaugurating Watchland in 1998, a little city dedicated to producing his watches, sold through a select distribution network and in single-brand shops in cities like Tokyo, Osaka, Geneva and Milan.

Caliber 2000

Watch with perpetual calendar, large and small chime and minute repeater, indications on double dial, 2000.

Gérald Genta

Left

Les Fantasies

Self-winding watch, with
a gold octagonal case and
a dial featuring Mickey Mouse,
circa 1990.

The Gérald Genta brand was founded in 1969 by the company namesake, one of the world's most celebrated wristwatch designers. Swiss, but with Piedmont origins, Genta had already created numerous models for the biggest names in the business, including Universal Genève's Polerouter, the Bulgari-Bulgari and a trio of sport models—Royal Oak, Nautilus and Ingenieur (for, respectively, Audemars Piguet, Patek Philippe and IWC)—that, in the 1970s,

Octo

Self-winding watch with jumping
hours, retrograde minutes,
retrograde calendar hand and
a rose gold case.

Imagination, creativity and a desire to amaze are the key components distinguishing watches by Gérald Genta, a leading manufacture in the production of extravagant luxury, pairing gold, diamonds and ... Mickey Mouse.

Grande Sonnerie

Multi-complication self-winding watch, with tourbillon, large and small chime, perpetual calendar and a platinum case, circa 1990.

revolutionized the way of experiencing watches. When Gérald Genta decided to step into the limelight working under his own name, he gave free reign to his creative energies, designing an array of watches united by a single common denominator: imagination. His surge of innovations included cases, dials and mechanisms, which were presented in collections like Octa, featuring an octagonal case and Gefica, inspired by three Italian friends (Gerani, Fissore and Canali) in search of an exclusive timepiece. Genta experimented with watch hands, transforming Mickey Mouse's arms into hour and minute indicators, boldly introducing cartoon characters into the world of luxury, but without neglecting the technical and spectacular aspect of mechanisms, introducing, in 1994 the Grande Sonnerie in celebration of the house's twenty-fifth anniversary. It was one of the most complicated wristwatches in the world, with eight grand complications and a stepped bezel, in an extremely limited edition of just a handful of exemplars. To celebrate its thirtieth anniversary, the house created a model that was similar but with the addition of a four-tone Westminster carillon. The most interesting developments of the 1990s include watches with jumping hours and retrograde minutes, produced using a patented system applied to cases in a variety of shapes. Ownership of Gérald Genta has changed hands twice: in 1996, the company was acquired by Hour Glass (an Asian investment group) and, in 2000, by Bulgari. Gérald Genta passed away in 2011 at the age of eighty.

Solo

Self-winding watch with jumping hours and retrograde minutes, retrograde calendar hand and a rose gold case.

Arena

Self-winding watch with jumping hours, retrograde minutes, retrograde calendar hand and a steel case.

One of the oldest Swiss manufactures, interested from the beginning in technical developments and masterful at creating solutions of major mechanical and aesthetic impact, from intense research and experimentation with quartz to a tourbillon with three gold bridges.

Girard-Perregaux

The origin of Girard-Perregaux, one of the oldest manufactures in Switzerland, dates to 1791, the year in which the horologist Jean François Bautte opened an atelier in Geneva. In 1856, Constant Girard, a horologist from La Chaux-de-Fonds, and his wife Marie Perregaux founded Girard-Perregaux, which acquired Bautte's business in 1906, inheriting its founding year and manufacturing excellence. One of the company's most famous designs was the Esmeralda, a spectacular tourbillon "sous Trois Ponts d'Or" ("with three gold bridges"), which was a prizewinner at the 1867 Paris Universal Exhibition and again in 1889. It was a timepiece of exceptional technical complexity, using gold as a fundamental element, including for the bridges that enclose the mechanism's mobile components. A capacity to approach timepieces with an innovating spirit led Constant Girard to develop one of history's first wristwatches: at

Italian Poster for the 1967 film, "The Graduate" (Il Laureato), starring Dustin Hoffman, Anne Bancroft and Katharine Ross.

Opposite
Laureato Evo3

Self-winding chronograph with perpetual calendar and a rose gold case.

Bottom
Laureato Evo3

Self-winding chronograph with a central minute counter, calendar and a steel case and bracelet.

Left
Laureato

Electronic quartz watch with date, lunar phases and zodiac, circa 1980.

Right
Laureato

Watch with an analog calendar at twelve o'clock and a gold and steel case and bracelet, 1984.

Laureato

Electronic quartz watch with a gold and steel case and bracelet, 1975.

Gyromatic

Automatic, non-circular watch with a Gyromatic winding system, a frequency of 36,000 vibrations/hour and a steel case and bracelet, 1970.

Integrated Circuit

Electronic quartz watch with a steel case, 1970. Above, a close-up of the dial, which recalls the design of integrated circuits.

Gyromatic

Automatic watch with a steel case, Gyromatic winding system and a chronometer certificate from the Observatory in Neuchâtel, 1967.

Girard-Perregaux then expanded its commercial presence in America and Asia, and moved its headquarters to Place Girardet 1, also in La Chaux-de-Fonds. The manufacture has always found this place to be favored with an extremely fertile and efficient productive fabric and it became the site, in 1999, of the Girard-Perregaux museum, housed in Villa Marguerite. The best-known models produced by Gerard-Perregaux include the Olimpico, a chronograph created for the Olympic Games,

the end of the nineteenth century, Emperor William I of Prussia, noting the company's watches at the international industrial exhibition in Berlin, ordered a large number of watches for German naval officers. The first exemplars, with a rudimentary leather strap and a robust grill protecting the crystal, were delivered in 1880. During the next century, the house's production was increasingly focused on satisfying the new way reading the time, or rather wearing the watch on the wrist instead of carrying it in one's waistcoat pocket.

Digital

Electronic quartz watch made of Makrolon (a synthetic material), with a LED time indicator, 1976.

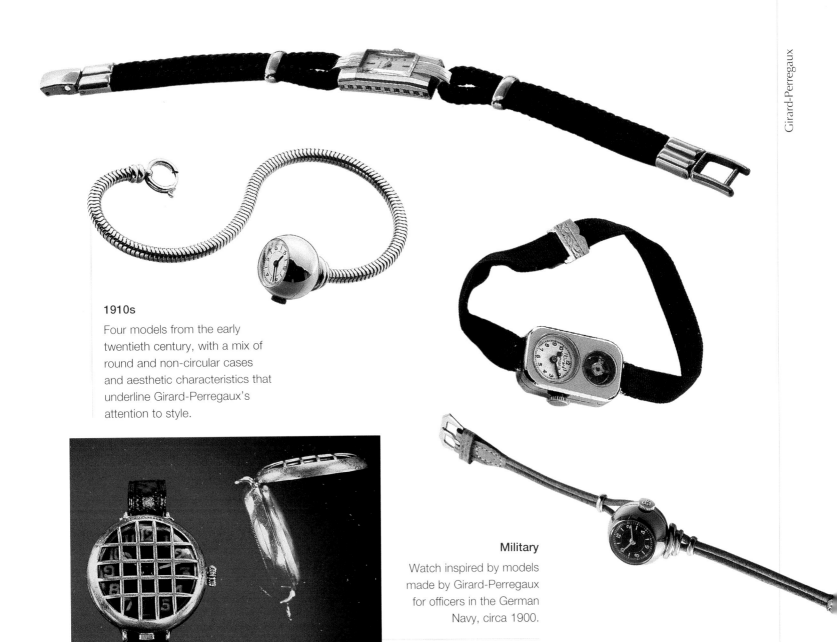

1910s

Four models from the early
twentieth century, with a mix of
round and non-circular cases
and aesthetic characteristics that
underline Girard-Perregaux's
attention to style.

Military

Watch inspired by models
made by Girard-Perregaux
for officers in the German
Navy, circa 1900.

updating the style of its case and dial as well as its technical solutions every four years, following the rhythm of the international sporting event. In the area of self-winding wristwatches, starting in 1935 Girard-Perregaux dedicated itself to technical research aimed to improve reliability and precision and culminating in the Gyromatic in 1957, the fruit of more than twenty years of experimentation. Anticipating future trends became one of Girard-Perregaux's distinctive traits, introducing the first high-frequency mechanical movement (36,000 vibrations per hour) in 1966.

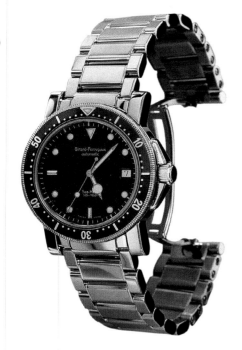

Sea-Hawk
Self-winding watch with
a steel and gold case and
bracelet, waterproof up
to 500 meters, 1989.

In 1969, the year when quartz was revolutionizing the world of horology, Girard-Perregaux set itself apart through the introduction of a 32.768 Hz mechanism, a frequency suited to that watch-type's functional and energy consumption principles. Thanks to the reliability of Girard-Perregaux's frequency, it became embraced as the universal standard for quartz watches. On the aesthetic front, in the 1970s the company presented the Laureato (the "graduate"), the name for which was suggested by the company's Italian importer. With a hexagonal bezel and an integrated bracelet, this model was a stunning success.

Vintage 1945
Manual-winding
watch with a
yellow gold case.

S.F. Foudroyante
Self-winding with a 1/8
second chronograph
and a rose gold case,
from a limited series
celebrating the Scuderia
Ferrari, 1999.

Sea-Hawk II
Self-winding watch with
power reserve and a steel
case and bracelet; waterproof
up to 300 meters.

n the decade that followed, Girard-Perregaux climbed to the highest heights of horological savoir-faire, reissuing the pocket watch version of the three gold bridges tourbillon in 1981, followed by a wristwatch variation of the same mechanism. The company later embarked on a revisitation of its house models overall, with a series of watches celebrating an important partnership signed with Ferrari in 1993. The Tribute to Ferrari collection included, among the rarest pieces, a rattrapante chronograph and the Ferrari F50, a chronograph with perpetual calendar, produced in a limited edition. In celebration of the ten-year anniversary of this partnership, the house introduced the Tribute to Enzo Ferrari, an incredible three gold bridge tourbillon, with chronograph and perpetual calendar. The house's sport watch horology was rounded out by the Sea Hawk, a collection characterized by the perfect watertightness of the case, the reissue of the Laureato and the WW.TC, a self-winding chronograph with a "world time" display of powerful visual impact. While the classic side of Girard-Perregaux timepieces was expressed in the Richeville, with a classic tonneau case, and the Vintage 1945, with an effectively updated old-fashioned style. In 2008, the French luxury group PPR became one of Girard-Perregaux's major shareholders.

Sous Trois Ponts d'Or

Tourbillon with Three Gold Bridges with a rose gold case, rose gold bridges for the self-winding mechanism and a skeleton movement, 2003.

Glashütte Original

G lashütte Original is inspired by the horology tradition that has distinguished the town of Glashütte (nestled among the Ore Mountains just a few kilometers from Dresden) since 1845. The timepieces created by Ferdinand Adolph Lange, Julius Assmann and Alfred Helwig, leading figures during a period of major technical and artistic development in the area and fed by the continuous training ensured by the German School of Horology in Glashütte, were among the most highly appreciated instruments for the measurement of time produced between the end of the nineteenth century and the beginning of the twentieth.

PanoRetroGraph

The first mechanical chronograph with a countdown function. Triple chime, platinum case; limited series of 50 pieces, 2001. Above, the PanoRetroGraph Caliber 60 manual-winding movement.

After the long 'hibernation' of the post-war period, many companies started flourishing again in Saxony, with products characterized by a distinctive "German made" style. In this context, Glashütte Original stood out for its absolute technical excellence.

Over its nearly two centuries of history, Glashütte suffered two periods of particular difficulty, both tied to war. In the period after World War I, the overall economic crisis led to a major slowdown, which companies in Glashütte were then able to overcome through the production of wristwatches, marine chronometers and precision instruments. After World War II, economic recovery was seriously threatened by the isolation from the West, caused by the division of Germany (Saxony and therefore also Glashütte found themselves in East Germany) and a forced tie to the Soviet Bloc, with horology companies being incorporated into the VEB Glashütter Uhrenbetriebe consortium. After German Reunification, the formerly state-owned companies were privatized and the Glashütte Original brand was

The new Glashütte Original manufacture.

Sport Evolution Chronograph

Self-winding chronograph with a steel case and bracelet.

Manual-Winding Karree

Perpetual calendar with a rose gold case. Below, Caliber 42, the watch's mechanical soul.

established in 1994 (later acquired in the year 2000 by the Swatch Group), introducing new quality standards and dedicating itself to developing a highly technical and innovative mechanism. The standard-bearers of this new period of German horology at Glashütte Original were the Julius Assmann 1 (1995), a tourbillon with perpetual calendar, the PanoRetroGraph (2001), the first mechanical chronograph with countdown, and models with fine Meissen porcelain dials.

From the wrists of American soldiers to those of
Elvis Presley and Hollywood film stars: since 1892,
Hamilton has represented stars and stripes horology,
producing models that stand out for their innovation,
technology and design.

Hamilton and the Asymmetrical Case

Left, self-winding Pacermatic, gold-
plated steel case, circa 1960.
Right, the Hamilton Ventura, the world's
first electronic watch, gold case, 1957.

Hamilton

Lancaster, Pennsylvania, 1892: American horology witnessed the birth of Hamilton, which, in 1893, produced a pocket model for the railroad industry, the Broadway Limited, with a degree of precision highly appreciated in an age when the efficiency and punctuality of trains was essential for the economic growth of the country. The debut of women's horology came in 1908, with the Lady Hamilton, a model that demonstrated the company's extraordinary flexibility in quickly adapting to market demand. This special capacity led Hamilton in the expression of its creative talent throughout the entire twentieth century.

Hamilton advertisement in Harper's Magazine: "The watch of railroad accuracy".

Four Famous Trains · · and the Famous Watch That Times Them

It's just as easy for you to have accurate time as it is for these railroad men. It's easier in fact, for your watch doesn't get the constant vibration their watches have to stand.

Railroad men and jewelers will endorse the Hamilton Watch—*every Hamilton*. There are no low-grade Hamiltons—no Hamiltons with less than 17 jewels—no Hamiltons that are not accurately adjusted before leaving the factory—no Hamiltons that are not guaranteed to give complete satisfaction to the user.

The Hamilton Watch combines the supreme qualities—accuracy, beauty and durability. Remember this when you buy a watch.

Over 75% of the value of a fine watch movement is *invisible*. It is the time and care and skill employed in putting it together, and in making the minute final adjustments, that constitute the difference between a fine watch movement and one which merely looks like it.

The story of the Hamilton will enable you to appreciate the good points of a high-grade watch. It will give you an accurate knowledge of what to look for in buying.

Write for Hamilton Watch Book, "The Timekeeper"

Let us send you a copy of this book. It illustrates and describes all Hamilton models for men and women and is full of interesting watch information. The lowest-priced Hamilton is a movement alone for $12.25 ($13.00 in Canada). The highest-priced Hamilton is our Masterpiece at $150.00 in 18k extra heavy gold case. Other Hamiltons at $25.00, $28.00, $40.00, $55.00, $90.00, $150.00, etc. All have Hamilton accuracy, beauty and durability Hamiltons are made in many models—in cased watches; also in movements alone which your jeweler can fit to your present watch case.

HAMILTON WATCH COMPANY, Dept. C, Lancaster, Pennsylvania

Hamilton Watch

"The Watch of Railroad Accuracy"

When writing to advertisers kindly mention Harper's Magazine.

Spectre

Electronic watch with a gold-plated asymmetrical case, circa 1950.

Victor III

Electronic watch with a gold-plated asymmetrical case, circa 1950.

Hamilton's partnership with the U.S. Army, which was one of the company's strong points, began in 1910, with models created to meet specific military requirements, while in the 1940s, during World War II, Hamilton produced more than one million watches for the US Armed Forces. Leaders of the American government's air, land, sea and space expeditions placed orders with the company, and Hamilton watches accompanied Admiral Byrd on his polar explorations and the Piccard brothers on the first flight beyond the confines of the stratosphere.

Performance reliability and aesthetics were the key characteristics of Hamilton production during the 1920s and 30s, with models like the Piping Rock of 1928, with a design that combined the circular and tonneau case shapes, an aesthetic mix that then inspired other models, like the Ardmore, Benton and Boulton.

The 1950s saw Hamilton in a position of technical superiority, unveiling the world's first electronic watch in 1957: this was the Ventura, a model with an asymmetrical case that resembled the fins of 1950s American cars. It was an innovative, avant-garde design and caught the eye of Elvis Presley, who wore it in a few scenes of the film "Blue Hawaii". This silver screen debut was followed by many others, starring on the wrists

Pulsar

The first digital watch, electronic quartz movement with a steel case and bracelet, 1970.

of Hollywood actors, as well as a special request for a watch for the filming of Stanley Kubrick's masterpiece "2001: Space Odyssey" in 1966.

In the race to electronic watches, Hamilton stood out in the 1970s for the Pulsar, the world's first digital watch. The lights on the dial launched a new way of reading the time, which was then adopted by the producers of quartz watches, in particular the Japanese. During that same period, Hamilton was acquired by SMH, now the Swatch Group, which contributed much to its development. Equipped with Swiss movements, Hamilton watches are divided into two lines inspired by the past: American Classics and the Khaki Collection, featuring watches that pair traditional aesthetics with contemporary taste. The reissues are complemented by new models for both men and wokmen, with special attention to the new functions introduced by new mechanisms. The Khaki models represent Hamilton's solid tie to military horology: sport models that usually feature dials with a rigorous graphic style and satin-finish cases. This strategy has been especially appreciated by connoisseurs and was rewarded with appearances in many films in the 1990s, including "Pearl Harbor", "Men in Black", "Lethal Weapon 4" and "Independence Day".

Piping Rock

Manual-winding watch with a steel case wedding the circle and the tonneau case shapes and a watch back engraved in honor of the Yankees' 1928 World Series triumph.

An advertisement publicizing the use of Hamilton watches for navigation.

Left
Khaki

Khaki Manual-winding watch with a steel case, fabric strap and black dial, circa 1940.

Center
US Navy Watch

Manual-winding watch with a steel case, circa 1940.

Right
Army Field

Manual-winding watch with a steel case, circa 1940.

Harry Winston

The "King of Diamonds" is also a refined producer of elegant timepieces marked by an unmistakable aesthetic and highly technical mechanisms. Its Opus collection, which debuted in the year 2000, was designed to safeguard and encourage top talent in the watch world.

The Harry Winston legend started in 1920 with the unveiling of the Premiere Diamond Company in Manhattan, the American jeweler's first business. But it was with the opening in 1932 of the Harry Winston Salon in Rockefeller Center in New York that the company became a leading light in the world of jewelry. Harry Winston revolutionized the concept of the diamond, no longer considered simply a precious object, but transformed into gem of natural beauty through meticulous attention to style and design. After boosting the allure of Hollywood stars and the international elite with its jewelry, Harry Winston made its horology debut in 1989. Its models were distinguished by a singular and inimitable glamor and were such a success that the house opened the Harry Winston Rare Timepieces facility in Geneva in 1998 and, in 2007, launched the Harry Winston Manufacture, also in Geneva. The company's commitment to high-end produc-

Opposite
Ocean Sport

Self-winding chronograph, waterproof up to 200 meters, case in zirconium and aluminum alloy and with a convex sapphire crystal.

Premier Ladies

Jewelry watch in white gold and diamonds, mother of pearl dial with diamond hour markers, self-winding movement.

tion has been fundamental from the start: steel was banished in favor of gold, platinum and, obviously, diamonds and precious stones. One of the brand's signature details, the three arches near the crown or horns, refer to the three architectural arches of the company's Fifth Avenue boutique in New York. From the premier of the Avenue line for women and the coquettish Talk to Me, Harry Winston—with Marilyn Monroe's famous declaration of love for the famed designer in the song "Diamonds are a Girl's Best Friend" hidden in a secret place in the case—to the Ocean and Midnight collections, designed, respectively, for use in sports and at black tie occasions. Launched in the year 2000, Opus, a joint venture between Harry Winston and the most interesting artists and artisans in contemporary horology, has become an essential reference for connoisseurs and collectors, who are intrigued by the initiative's aspiration to redefine the way of indicating time through mechanical imagination.

Ocean Triple Retrograde

Self-winding chronograph with eccentric, retrograde display of seconds, minutes and hours, rose gold case, waterproof up to 100 meters.

Hermès

Opposite
Heure "H"
Quartz watch with a white
gold case, mother of pearl
dial and alligator strap.

Hermès' debut in the world of horology dates to the end of the 1920s, when interest began to develop at its location on Rue du Faubourg Saint-Honoré in Paris in timepieces, which were then produced over the following decades on an occasional basis and in collaboration with the top

Heure "H"
Watch with a quartz movement, steel case and diamond encrusted bezel.

Synonymous with elegance and understated luxury, Hermès represents a world of refined accessories inspired by the sporting disciplines. In horology, the name of the French house is tied to precious models and functionally and aesthetically innovative designs, with straps of the finest quality leather, in true Hermès style.

names in the field. Nearly fifty years passed before the house decided to open an independent watch business, founding La Montre Hermès in 1978 in Bienne, Switzerland. The company's watch production was

Kelly Clochette

Padlock-shaped pendant watch, drawing on the eponymous collection of Hermès purses; quartz movement.

Harnais

Orange and black versions of a watch distinctive for its prominent leather strap with exposed stitching; quartz movement.

committed from the start to the same high quality standards that had been introduced in all of the other areas of Hermès activity since 1837: precious materials or steel, simple mechanisms of unwavering reliability and leather straps designed to enhance the qualities of their material, offering a unique tactile sensation.

The brand's designs for women were of particular aesthetic impact, especially those of the Heure H line, where the house initial is transformed into a case packed with personality and usually embellished with diamonds set into the bezel. Harnais, Nomade, Belt, Glissade and Kelly (the latter named after the eponymous Hermès cult bag) are just a few of the models introduced in those years in the area of sport timepieces, counterbalanced by the Dressage line, launched in 2003 and distinctive for its mechanical excellence.

Dressage

Watch with a rose gold case, Swiss movement with lunar phases and retrograde calendar.

Hublot

Classic
Self-winding watch with a yellow gold case and natural rubber strap, circa 1990.

The brand's birth certificate is dated 1980, the year in which the Italian watchmaker Carlo Crocco founded MDM (which later became Hublot SA) in Geneva, a company that quickly came to be identified with its star watch model, the Hublot. This was an aesthetically revolutionary design, pairing a precious gold case with a natural rubber strap. A combination, that is, in blatant contrast with the traditional classicism of the models most representative of that period, one during which Swiss horology was recovering from the shock of the Japanese quartz revolu-

Classic Fusion Tourbillon Squelette
Manual-winding titanium watch, limited series of 99 pieces.

Gold and natural rubber were the includible combination for Hublot's debut in the 1980s, a "creative sacrilege" that became a must of wristwatch elegance and style, embodied in a timepiece that wedded technology to a timeless aesthetic.

tion, transforming the watch in less than a decade into a true status symbol. The Hublot brand is about the desire to amaze, developing an innovative concept of sport horology through a product line with a big personality and strong character, marked by a savvy combination of technology and aesthetics, formal purity and respect for technique.

The name "Hublot" derives from the shape of the case, which was inspired by ship portholes (the French word for "porthole" is "hublot"), with a bezel attached by twelve titanium screws that also function as the hour markers for the hands. It was an immediate success. The watch with a natural rubber strap became an object of desire among connoisseurs and its history has been characterized by an almost silent evolution. Its style has remained all but unchanged, while some of its complications and elements of the case have been modified. Over the years, the company has passed from covered models in its Classic and Elegant lines to dials decorated with engraving or enamel designs; from the first models

Classic Couvercle
Self-winding watch
with a steel case
and hand-engraved click
open cover, circa 2000.

with an electronic quartz mechanism to self-winding designs; and from chronographs and GMT to models with waterproof and diving cases. The brand's aesthetic was radically renewed in 2005, when Jean-Claude Biver launched the Big Bang, a new Hublot horology concept with an innovative, aesthetically appealing case creating a "fusion" between steel and ceramic, Kevlar and gold, and titanium and natural rubber. In 2008, Hublot was acquired by the LVMH group.

Left
Plongeur Professional

Self-winding watch with
a steel case, waterproof
up to 300 meters,
circa 1990.

Right
Classic

Electronic quartz watch,
enamel decorated dial,
circa 1990.

GMT

Self-winding watch
with dual time zone and
a steel case,
circa 1990.

Classic Fusion Racing Grey
Self-winding watch with
calendar, 45-millimeter gold
case, Racing Grey dial, strap
in alligator sewn over natural
rubber.

Bottom
Classic Fusion Chrono
Self-winding chronograph
with two timers and 42-hour
power reserve, 45-millimeter
gold case, opaque black dial,
black natural rubber strap.

The evolution of the brand's production, marked by aggressive shapes and increasingly precise mechanisms, has been expressed in collections like Big Bang, Classic Fusion and King Power, where the strong character of technological materials is paired with an all-black aesthetic, with the ceramic case transformed into a jewel with gold and diamond detailing. The limited series became a Hublot specialty, providing a way of celebrating the biggest sports stars of the moment (the basketball player Dwyane Wade, the Jamaican sprinter Usain Bolt and the beloved soccer player, Diego Armando Maradona), the world's most famous soccer teams and the exciting world of Formula 1. The house's partnership with Ferrari, which began in 2011, has also resulted in a series of limited editions, with cases in carbon fiber, titanium and magic gold, a special, exclusive Hublot alloy combining ceramic and gold, for increased strength and unprecedented shine.

Big Bang

Self-winding mechanical
chronograph with a red gold case,
black ceramic dial attached with
titanium screws, lateral inserts
in composite resin, carbon dial,
shaped natural rubber strap,
sapphire glass black revealing
a movement designed in-house.

A German-speaking Swiss house, IWC has dedicated itself from the start to practical innovation and technological refinement, revolutionizing the method used to construct watches and contributing, with mechanically exceptional pieces, to the progress of watchmaking technics.

IWC

"Probus Scafusiae" or "Good products from Schaffausen": the house motto is the perfect summary of the philosophy guiding the production of its timepieces. IWC (the International Watch Co.) was founded in 1868 in Schaffausen, far from the traditional centers of Swiss watchmaking, by an American, Florentine Ariosto Jones, and an entrepreneur, Johann Heinrich Moser. Production was initially focused on pocket watches with the Jones caliber, a high precision, stem-wind mechanism.

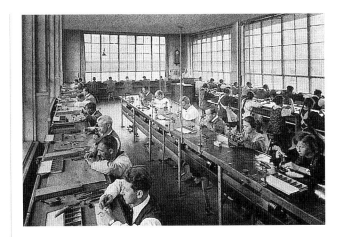

A photograph from 1920 of the IWC workshop where the final checks were carried out on its watches.

Around 1875, IWC became a limited company and ownership passed to Schaffausen Handelsbank. Five years later, the company was acquired by Johannes Rauschenbach-Vogel, whose family would continue to lead the company for many years. In 1890, IWC produced the first Grande Complication pocket watch, which had more than 1,300 mechanical parts.

Big Pilot's Watch

Self-winding watch in steel with calendar and power reserve indicator.

Opposite
Military

Left, Big Pilot's Watch, 1940.
Right, the antimagnetic
Mark XI, 1948.

UTC

Self-winding watch in steel with digital second time zone indicator.

In the twentieth century, the company introduced its first wrist models, made with reduced-scale movements designed for pocket watches. In the same period, the company began supplying watches to the British Royal Navy and the German Imperial Navy, also providing the Berlin tram company with a series of nonmagnetic watches, featuring a special structure for maintaining normal functionality even in the presence of the magnetic fields generated by electric motors. In 1929, Ernst Jakob Homberger bought IWC. At the end of the 1930s, IWC presented what would become one of its leading models, the Portuguese. The house had received a special order from Rodriguez e Texeira, a Portuguese watch importer, requesting a steel model with a large diameter case and a highly legible dial. To meet this request, the IWC designers decided to use a manual-winding mechanism created for pocket watches

but built inside a wristwatch case. This singular model was baptized the Portuguese, after its market of destination.

In 1940, during World War II, IWC began producing a series of high precision, robust models for the military, the so-called "Fliegeruhr" line, featuring black dials and luminescent hour markers, so that the watch could be consulted even in problematic light conditions. The case was generously sized and paired a solid structure with characteristics designed to make the piece highly resistant and protect it from every kind of external strain. One of the best-known models from this line was the manual-winding Mark XI. In 1950, IWC unveiled its interpretation of the self-winding mechanism, featuring an innovative winding device worked out by Albert Pellaton, the house's technical director, who designed a simple

Ingenieur

Watch with gold case and movement protected from magnetic fields, circa 1950.

Ingenieur

Self-winding watch with a steel case and bracelet and protection from magnetic fields, circa 1970.

Ingenieur

Right, self-winding watch made in 2005, fifty years after the debut of the first Ingenieur. Below, a chronograph version.

Portuguese

Self-winding chronograph in the gold and steel versions with an alligator strap.

Portuguese

Seven-day power reserve, rose gold, limited series of 750 pieces, 2000.

Portuguese

Mechanical watch in steel with IWC Pocket Watch Caliber 74, circa 1940.

Portuguese

Manual-winding rattrapante chronograph with a rose gold case.

and reliable double-pawl winding system, which would be applied to the Ingenieur and Yacht Club models of the 1950s. In the area of technological development, IWC and other companies participated in the creation of Caliber Beta 21, the first Swiss quartz movement produced on an industrial scale, which started being used in the 1970s in an attempt to counter, unfortunately in vain, the advance of Japanese quartz production.

Interested in pursuing new directions, in 1978, IWC linked its name to that of Ferdinand A. Porsche. This partnership, which would last for more than twenty years, resulted in the brand Porsche Design by IWC, which produced avant-garde, essential models featuring solutions appreciated by those looking to go beyond classic horology formulas. Examples are the titanium case and integrated buttons of the Chrono

Titan, the underwater pressure resistance of the Ocean 2000 of 1982 (the first entirely titanium sport model) and the pairing of time indicators and compass points in the Bussola model. 1978 was also the year in which IWC was acquired by the Mannesmann group: under the leadership of Günter Blümlein, the company prepared itself to take on the renaissance of the mechanical watch with new ideas and sufficient economic resources.

In 1985, IWC and Jaeger-LeCoultre joined forces to develop a perpetual calendar model for which all of the indicators were regulated by the crown and which featured a four-digit digital year display. The prestigious mechanical base was set into a yellow gold, white gold or high-tech ceramic case and thus was born the Da Vinci perpetual calendar chronograph, an epoch-changing watch for the Sciaffusa compa-

Porsche Design

Watch with a lift-up case and professional compass, circa 1978.

Porsche Design

Astronomical chronograph with integrated buttons, circa 1980.

Porsche Design

Chronograph with a titanium case and bracelet, circa 1980.

ny and later produced in rattrapante and tourbillon variants. The company's run of pre-eminent models reached its apex in the 1990s with two multi-complication watches: the Grande Complication followed by the Destriero Scafusiae, in celebration of the house's 125th anniversary. For an idea of the refinement of these two masterpieces, consider that the Grande Complication was a perpetual calendar and minute repeater chronograph with 9 hands and 654 components. While the Destriero, although lacking the Grande Complication's self-winding mechanism, stepped up the complications introduced in its illus-

GST

Self-winding mechanical chronograph with a titanium case and bracelet.

Mark XV

Self-winding watch with central seconds, calendar and an antimagnetic steel case.

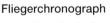

Fliegerchronograph

Aviator's self-winding chronograph with a steel case and dual calendar.

In 2000, IWC was bought by the Richemont group. The company's production of high quality pieces continued, and new models were introduced that reinforced the strong focus on technical and technological research that had distinguished the house since 1868. The Portuguese, the "outsize" model from the 1930s, was reissued in 1993 in a limited edition to celebrate the company's 125th anniversary and produced in a wide range of variants, including two chronographs—simple and rattrapante—that were very well-received by connoisseurs. The design was developed into two new series, the Portuguese Automatic 2000, which brought back the

Grande Complication

Self-winding watch with minute repeater, perpetual calendar, lunar phases and chronograph, 1990.

trious predecessor, adding a rattrapante chronograph and a splendid tourbillon in a titanium case. IWC flanked exclusive models designed for a highly discriminating clientele with appealing watches like the Fliegerchronograph and the Doppelcronograph, chronographs inspired by the aviator style of the past: black dial, anti-reflection crystal and luminescent hands and hour markers. These models opened the way for a successful collection of military-style watches, including the UTC (with dual time zone), the Mark XII, the Mark XV and, more recently, the Big Pilot's Watch, with eight-day power reserve. In 1997, the company launched the GST line (gold, steel and titanium were the metals used for the case and bracelet) to replace the Porsche Design by IWC models.

Electronic

Da Vinci gold watch with revolutionary Beta 21 quartz movement, 1969.

Portofino

Self-winding mechanical watch in steel with date, small seconds and eight-day power reserve display.

Pellaton self-winding movement, and the Portuguese Perpetual Calendar, which paired the model's mechanism with a perpetual calendar derived from the historic Da Vinci design, introducing a patented system for indicating the lunar phases. In 2005, the house reissued the Ingenieur, fifty years after its debut, with a self-winding mechanism and chronograph in a powerful concentration of technology featuring a supplementary internal case in soft iron designed to resist magnetic fields, an integrated bracelet (as with the chronograph buttons) as well as technical versions in titanium.

Portuguese

Left, three versions—yellow gold, platinum and rose gold—of the self-winding watch with perpetual calendar and lunar phases.

Thus began a phase during which each year the creative department has selected one collection from IWC's methodically organized catalog to revamp for the Salon International de la Haute Horlogerie. 2006 was the year of the Pilot's Watches, which were slightly increased in size and special editions were unveiled dedicated to Antoine de Saint-Exupery, the romantic World War II pilot who gave the world "The Little Prince", a book beloved by generations of readers, young and old. The new Da Vinci line, produced in various chronograph and perpetual calendar models, debuted the next year, an important time for the Schaffausen house, which opened a corporate museum on the banks of the Rhine, with a wall of timepieces telling the story of the brand. The 140th anniversary of the company was celebrated in 2008 with the Vintage Collection, six pieces representing IWC's design and manufacturing excellence. The revamping of the product families started up again in 2009, with the new Aquatimer models, followed by the unveiling of unprecedented designs in recent years, accompanying the comprehensive updating of the Portuguese, Portofino and Pilot's Watches families.

Portuguese Automatic

Self-winding watch with seven-day power reserve indicator, rose gold case and alligator strap.

1

Aquatimer Galapagos Edition

Self-winding chronograph, waterproof up to 120 meters with a steel case covered in black vulcanized natural rubber.

2

Top Gun Miramar

Chronograph with polished ceramic case and military fabric strap; Pellaton self-winding system.

3

Top Gun Big Pilot

Watch with over-sized steel case and knurled crown; Pellaton self-winding system.

4

Top Gun Chronograph

Self-winding chronograph with flyback function, ceramic case with internal protection from magnetic effects.

1

2

4

3

Hands, heart and eye: the three-part key to transforming a watch into a masterpiece distinguished for its mechanical beauty. And also the philosophy of the men who transformed Jaeger-LeCoultre into a manufacture distinguished for its high stylistic appeal.

Jaeger-LeCoultre

A manufacture with a double name, as is common in the world of watches, Jaeger-LeCoultre took its current moniker in 1937, as part of the merging of two separate businesses founded in two different time periods, with the Parisian Jaeger joining the "old" LeCoultre, established in 1833 in Le Sentier, on the Swiss side of the Vallée de Joux. Driven by an exceptional talent, its founder, Charles-Antoine LeCoultre, specialized in producing components for watch mechanisms, introducing new fabrication methods and innovative tools, like the "millionmeter", a tool that he invented in 1844 for measuring one one-thousandth of a millimeter, which permitted a degree of precision almost absolute for the time. The quality of his production of pocket watch components led LeCoultre to become the supplier of the most prestigious names in horology, including Patek Philippe, Audemars Piguet, Vacheron Constantin, Cartier and Girard-Perregaux. Toward the end of the nineteenth century, the first LeCoultre branded watches appeared. The company's technical achievements are numerous: Caliber 145 of 1903, the world's

Print advertisement for the Reverso, 1983.

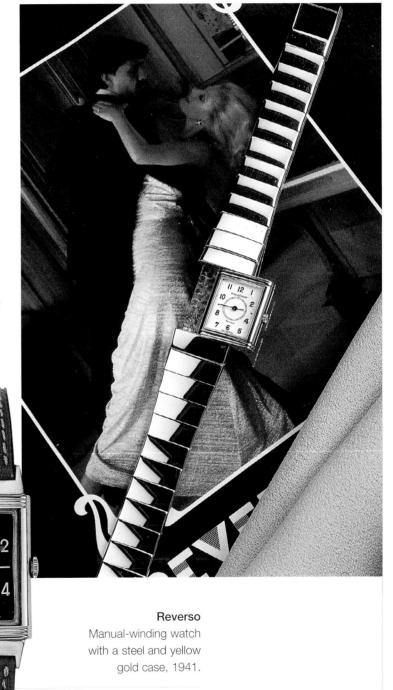

Reverso
Manual-winding watch with a steel and yellow gold case, 1941.

Opposite
Reverso
Three variations of the Reverso, the watch with a rotating case patented by Jaeger-LeCoultre in 1931.

thinnest pocket-watch movement (1.38 mm); the manual-winding Caliber 101 (1929), also called the "2 ligne" (in reference to its width in millimeters converted into the "ligne parisienne"), which is still today the smallest watch mechanism ever made, comprising ninety-eight elements in a space measuring 4.84 x 14 mm (and weighing about one gram).

In the early twentieth century, Jacques-David LeCoultre, Charles-Antoine's grandson, met Edmond Jaeger, and the two began a fruitful collaboration that led to the merging of their businesses. It was a period of exponential growth for the wristwatch and well represented by LeCoultre and Jaeger models. The Duoplan dates to 1926 and featured a rectangular movement and components arranged on two levels. In a brilliant marketing move, dealers were asked to provide a series of services during the warranty period, specifically to replace the move-

Charles-Antoine LeCoultre. Below, the millionometer, a device invented by LeCoultre to accurately measure a micrometer.

Power Reserve

Self-winding watch with power reserve indicator and a yellow gold case, circa 1940.

Futurematic

Self-winding watch with power reserve indicator at nine o'clock and small seconds at three o'clock; case in yellow gold, 1953.

ment, dial and hands should they malfunction, and the watch itself came with Lloyd's of London insurance coverage against theft, loss and irreparable damage.

The sophistication of the company's mechanisms was an inspiration to its designers, who created jewelry watches worn by the most glamorous women of the age: examples include the Duoplan, the 2 Ligne, the Etrier, with slender, elongated horns, and, finally, the Mystérieuse, with two indicators attached to concentric, rotating disks instead of the traditional hour and minute hands. In the same period, and specifically 1931, Jaeger-LeCoultre unveiled a model that expressed the height of the brand's excellence in wristwatch design: the Reverso. The watch was designed on the suggestion of César de Trey, a dealer specialized in luxury brands, including Jaeger-LeCoultre. During a busi-

Jaeger-LeCoultre

1950s print advertisement for Jaeger-LeCoultre watches.

Memovox Polaris

Self-winding watch with alarm and a waterproof steel case, circa 1960.

ness trip in Asia, the English officers stationed in India asked him for a watch that could stand up to polo matches, since the frequent impacts sustained during game play often resulted in broken dials or mechanisms. The only solution was to produce a model with a case that could be turned back to front. This idea was transformed into a watch by LeCoultre, with the engineer René-Alfred Chauvot working out the design for the special case. Patent request no. 712.868 was filed on March 4, 1931 at

the Board of Trade and Industry in Paris, with the description, "watch able to slide within its support and turn over completely on its axis". The special aspect of the model is its case, which is fastened to a support. The back, which initially reversed to protect the dial, became a field for personalization, from engraved initials to coats-of-arms, complex designs and miniature enamels.

The model's initial success was followed by a long hazy period. The decisive turning point was linked to Giorgio Corvo, who had long been the Italian Jaeger-LeCoultre dealer and who, in 1972, asked if he could rescue the two-hundred steel-case Reversos that had been abandoned in the company's stockrooms. In the years that followed, the house developed different formats for the cases and applied various complications, including tourbillon, minute repeater, chronograph and perpetual calendar, which expanded to range of the Jaeger-LeCoultre signature model.

Yet the fame of the manufacture did not depend wholly on the Reverso. In fact, its creations exalted the technical expertise and inventiveness of its designers: complete calendars with lunar phases, inserted in round or non-circular cases, and watches like the Geophysic (equipped with a special nonmagnetic soft iron inner case, this model was used on board the submarine Nautilus during its journey under the ice cap of the North Pole) and the Futurematic. The company's most characteristic model was the Memovox, an extremely practical mechanical alarm wristwatch, produced in a wide range of variations (it debuted with a manual-winding

Reverso 60°
Manual-winding watch
with power reserve,
calendar, and a rose gold
case; limited edition
of 500 pieces in
celebration of the debut
of the Reverso, 1991.

Reverso Calendar
Manual-winding watch
with retrograde calendar,
lunar phases and a yellow
gold case; prototype
that never went into
production, 1938.

Reverso Tourbillon
Manual-winding watch with tourbillon and a rose gold case; limited series of 500 pieces, 1993.

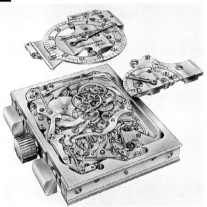

Reverso Chronographe Rétrograde
Manual-winding watch with chronograph, rose gold case, arrangement of indications on the dual dial; limited edition of 500 pieces, 1994.

Reverso Minute Repeater
Manual-winding watch with minute repeater and a rose gold case; limited series of 500 pieces, 1994.

movement in 1950, while the 1956 Memovox was also available with a self-winding device). As for company matters, Roger LeCoultre was the last of the family to head the business: in 1969, the house was acquired by Henry and Barbara Favre, who ceded ownership to the luxury watch group Mannesmann in 1978. In 2000, the company was acquired by the Richemont Group.

The 1980s and 90s saw the return of the brand in grand style, with the Géographique, a "world time" model that paired immediacy of legibility with a discrete, elegant style; the Master Series, with a round case that took center stage for its refinement and the versatility of the complications used; and the debut of the Compressor line, inspired by an exquisite Memovox model with three crowns from the 1960s (in addition to the winding and time regulating crown and the alarm crown, this design also featured a crown for operating the chapter ring

Etrier
Manual-winding
watch, 1935.

when underwater). The Jaeger-LeCoultre manufacture has a comprehensive presence in every market sector, also producing table clocks and mantle clocks, standing out among which is the Atmos, invented by Jean-Léon Reutter at the end of the 1920s and run with a movement that "lives on air", since it gets its energy from temperature variations. The Atmos does not require any kind of winding, just "a little air" to move its gears: a unique bit of magic with a brilliant mechanical arrangement based on the idea of using the factor of thermal expansion—of a gas or a liquid—to move the clock hands.

The smallest
The world's smallest
manual-winding watch,
with Caliber 101, the
world's smallest mechanical
movement, with a white gold
and diamond case.

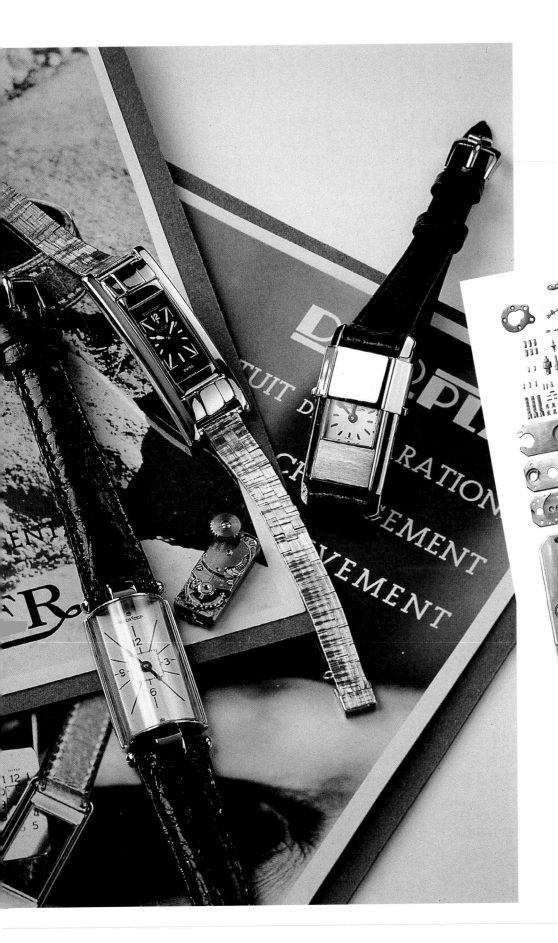

**Woman according
to Jaeger-LeCoultre**

Three Jaeger-LeCoultre
women's watches from
the 1920s.

Caliber 101

A technical design
with the smallest
manual-winding
mechanism in the
world, designed in
1929 by the Jaeger-
LeCoultre manufacture.

Hybris Mechanica à Grande Sonnerie

In white gold with jumping hours, Westminster carillon, minute repeater, tourbillon, perpetual calendar and power reserve indicator.

Reverso Grande Complication à Tryptique

In platinum with eighteen functions displayed on the two dials of the rotating case and the frame; movement comprising around 700 elements.

Gyrotourbillon

In platinum with spherical tourbillon, power reserve and equation of time indicator and perpetual indication of the date and months.

Duomètre à Chronographe

In rose gold with power reserve indicator for the watch and the chronograph, two independent barrels and a foudroyante (flying seconds) hand; manual-winding mechanical movement.

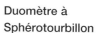

Duomètre à Sphérotourbillon

In rose gold with dual time zone, calendar and seconds; tourbillon that rotates on two axes: the axis of the rotation of the cage and the axis of the cage; manual-winding mechanical movement.

The first years of the new millennium started off with a crescendo of mechanical masterpieces, in the area of grand complications as well as that of everyday models. For the horology elite, the house released the Gyrotourbillon 1, with the Jaeger-LeCoultre Caliber 177, made up of a full 679 elements. Featuring a perpetual calendar with a dual retrograde indicator (the relative hands move on a graduated sector: once they reach the last division, they go back to their departure point), it also displayed the equation of time. But it was the absolutely unprecedented spherical tourbillon that carried the Gyrotourbillon 1 to a new dimension of wristwatch mechanics. Pre-eminence was likewise achieved by the Reverso Grande Complication à Triptyque, which used the surfaces provided by the reversible case to distribute

Grande Reverso Ultra Thin Tribute to 1931

Manual-winding mechanical watch with a slender 2.94-millimeter movement; steel case and alligator strap.

Grande Reverso Lady Ultra Thin

Manual-winding mechanical watch with a steel, diamond-encrusted case, silver-plated dial and guilloché decoration.

the information from the perpetual calendar, run by a single mechanism, on three dials. Its partnership with Aston Martin, the British luxury car brand, led Jaeger-LeCoultre to explore new frontiers. The AMVox2 of 2005 is a singular example, with a case that, through an ingenious system, becomes a practical element, since, with its movements inside a special support, it replaces the chronograph buttons. In 2008, the Master Duomètre introduced the Dual Wing concept, a new idea in watch design. Two mechanisms, synchronized by a single regulator and with an independent winding device, ensure the best possible chronometer precision while the complications are in use.

Weems and **Lindbergh**

Vintage exemplars of the
Weems, designed in the
1920s, and the Hour Angle,
conceived, based on the
preceding model, by the flight
pioneer Charles Lindbergh, the
hero of the first transatlantic
flight, piloting the Spirit of St.
Louis. Facing page, close-ups
the two models' case and dial,
circa 1930.

A house distinguished for its varied approach to horology, Longines is a leader in aviation timepieces, precision timing for the world of sports, innovation and glamor, producing models full of fascination and steeped in mechanical tradition.

Longines

S t. Imier, 1832: Auguste Agassiz opens an atelier that, thirty years later, under the leadership of his grandson Ernest Francillon, would become a true manufacture, producing every single component of its watches. The company, which took the name "Longines" in 1867 (with reference to the location of its new facility), expanded commercially, reaching all the way to the flourishing American market, and, starting in 1879, participated in the prestigious chronometry competitions organized by Swiss and European astronomy observatories, time and time again receiving recognition for the precision and structural exactness of its designs.

I n 1905, Longines began producing wristwatches, and, in 1912, for the Federal Gymnastics Competition in Basel, developed a self-winding chronometer that used an innovative electromagnetic system. The timing of sports events reached its experimental apex in the period after World War II: in 1952, in Oslo, Longines was the official timekeeper for the sixth Olympic Winter Games, a role that it would return to again and again.

With strong technical expertise in the areas of chronometry and chronography, Longines understood the importance of aviation for the advancement of civilization, and actively participated in the explorations carried out during the pioneering period of powered flight, ventures that were of tremendous fascination to the greater public. Starting in the 1920s, Longines timepieces were selected for many of the history-making feats of modern aviation. The most famous was Charles Augustus Lindbergh's 1927 transatlantic flight from New York to Paris in 33 hours and 39 minutes, on board the Spirit of St. Louis. Longines worked with Lindbergh himself to create what would become one of its most famous models: the Hour Angle. This watch integrated the model designed by Philippe

LONGINES

MESURE LE TEMPS

An advertising poster designed by René Bleuer, 1945.

Comet

In this design, the hours and minutes are indicated by an arrow and a dot; steel case and manual-winding movement, circa 1970. To the side, a close-up of the dial, distinctive for its bright colors.

Serge Manzon

Watches with silver cases. Collection by the French designer Serge Manzon, circa 1970.

Feuille d'Or

Electronic quartz watch with an extremely thin gold case, circa 1980.

Vanhorn Weems, a professor at the Naval Academy in Annapolis, with added functions and graduations, simplifying the position calculations and making it possible use the hands to display the hour angle, measured between the observer's meridian and that of a given celestial body. Longines continued developing mechanisms, presenting extra-thin calibers, chronographs and other complicated calibers, while at the same time paying close attention to aesthetics, especially in the 1960s and 70s, when the wristwatch was being interpreted by top designers. New lines and solutions were introduced, some focused on the slenderness of the gold case, some on volumes. For others still, color was the star of the dial.

Over the years, Longines has maintained its close tie to tradition and classicism, debuting collections like DolceVita, Flagship, Heritage and Evidenza, which draw on the genetic heritage of the house, emphasizing the refinement of the brand's style.

Les Elégantes

Modern reissue of precious watches from the 1920s, brought back in a limited series of fifty pieces, 2002.

Evidenza

Watches inspired by the lines of the 1920s, in the "three sphere" version or variants with complicated mechanisms.

Lorenz

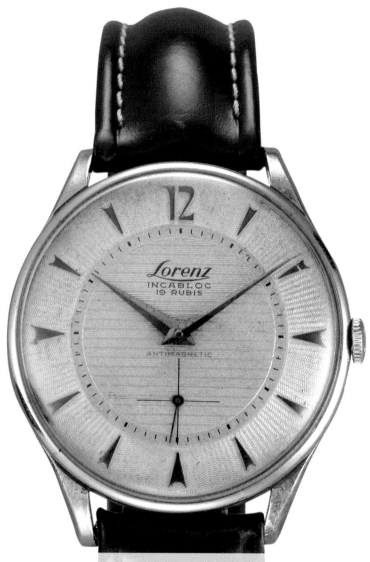

Incabloc

Watch with a steel case, manual-winding movement and shock resistant Incabloc device, circa 1970.

L orenz is one of the most fascinating brands in Italian wristwatch production. It all began in 1934, in Milan, where the founder, Tullio Bolletta, opened a workshop, four years later moving from his first location to a space on Via Montenapoleone, which later became the Lorenz boutique. In 1951, the company decided to work in direct collaboration with Swiss partners, using exclusively developed calibers. In addition to its wristwatch production, the company was involved in other interesting activity in the horological sphere, and thanks to partnerships

Theatro
Self-winding chronograph in steel with power reserve.

Emblematic of the Italian contribution to the world of horology, Lorenz has always represented a practical and reassuring vision of watches, with excellent value for price and a creative approach in step with market trends and the interests of connoisseurs.

Montenapoleone

Women's watch in steel
with a quartz movement,
circa 1980.

Montenapoleone

Men's watch in steel
and gold plate, self-
winding movement,
circa 1980.

Gold

Women's manual-
winding watch in
yellow gold,
circa 1950.

Elegance

Men's manual-
winding watch
in gold plate,
circa 1960.

with celebrated designers, Lorenz table clocks became well known in the furnishing sphere. Examples are the Static model, designed by Richard Sapper and winner of the Compasso d'Oro in 1960, and the company's collaboration in 1986 with the Memphis group, which led to the Neos brand, specializing in objects with a high design quotient.

The company's continuous expansion was always focused on the Italian market, but starting in the 1990s, Lorenz began following an internationalization plan that brought its watches to countries throughout Europe and the Middle East as well as Australia. The brand's most famous product lines include the Theatro, Montenapoleone, Sporting Club, Acapulco and Torneo wristwatch collections.

The secret of the house's success is unquestionably tied to its brilliance in maintaining an easy, familiar style in spite of its achievement of high sales figures, which has required the company to adopt a highly efficient and organized structure. In September 2003, Lorenz was named a "Historic Business" by the City of Milan, a titled conferred to the company by the Chamber of Industrial, Artisan and Agricultural Commerce of Milan.

A creative Lorenz print ad from the 1960s.

Louis Vuitton

Tambour V

Women's diamond and gold watch, with the celebrated "V" of the French house on its dial.

Opposite from left:
Tambour Voyagez

Self-winding chronograph in steel with tachymetric scale and twenty-four hour indicator.

Tambour Répétition Minutes

Manual-winding watch in white gold with dual time zone, 100 hour power reserve indicator and minute repeater.

Tambour Spin Time Joaillerie

White gold and diamond watch with self-winding movement and cube-shaped markers that rotate to mark the hour.

A leader in the production of luxury leather goods, in 1999, Louis Vuitton decided to develop a collection of sport watches, creating a line highly acclaimed by watch connoisseurs.

ouis Vuitton is one of the most famous leather goods and travel accessories brands in the world. Its story began in Paris in 1854 and the brand is distinguished for its widespread presence on five continents, with boutiques that captivate as much for their style as for their stunning locations, always in the center of most important shopping streets. The launching of the timepiece division dates to the company's more recent history, specifically 1991. After three years of experimentation in search of the perfect form, it released the Tambour model in 2002. A model with great style, it is distinguished for its unmistakable lines, which elegantly interpret the concept of sophisticated sport watches, perfect in women's versions and suited to hosting complicated movements. The center of the dial is often decorated with the flower design that has symbolized the house since 1896, or the company's interlacing initials, L and V, one of the best-loved symbols in international fashion. The Tambour Tourbillon Monogram was one of the first models with a mechanism of significant structural refinement, featuring a case with a conical shape, its diameter decreasing from the watch-back toward the bezel. This design was repeated in the next variation, a Tambour that took on a wide range of functional challenges, including dual time zone and a chronograph for measuring regatta times, in homage to the partnership between Louis Vuitton and the 1983 America's Cup. In 2011, the company acquired La Fabrique du Temps, an atelier specialized in producing high-end calibers, underlining the brand's dedication to research and development and continuing in the direction of technical and technological exclusivity.

MB&F

MB&F is a creative brand, embodying a reactionary and Renaissance approach to horology. Maximilian Büsser has transformed the concept of watch design, bringing together groups of artisans, who become "friends" of the brand (the name MB&F itself stands for "Maximilian Büsser and Friends").

Horological Machine N°1
In rose gold with a self-winding movement equipped with a "space hatchet" rotor, hours on the left dial, minutes and power reserve on the right dial and a tourbillon in the center; limited series of ten pieces.

Opposite
Horogical Machine N°3 – Frog
PVD-coated zirconium case with a "three-dimensional" sapphire crystal movement with hours, minutes and seconds displayed on rotating aluminum dials inserted in a sapphire glass dome (see inset image above); limited series of 18 pieces.

The principle behind MB&F, conceived by the original and independent mind of Maximilian Büsser, is based on the idea of involving artisans, artists and other professionals in a unique friendship, joining together to create unprecedented, innovative, extreme timepieces.

Product-oriented but also and above all a communications man, Büsser started his career at Jaeger-LeCoultre and Harry Winston Rare Timepieces, then decided to strike out on his own and create his own brand. He launched his start-up in 2005, concentrating on refining the network of friends that would lead to the creation of the first model, the HM1. The name stands for Horological Machine N°1 and the model is a wristwatch that expresses the passion, lucid madness and talent of the company's founder. The horizontal "figure 8"-shaped case houses a central tourbillon, with hours and minutes positioned on the four separate and distinct dials. It has a self-winding movement (the rotor is decorated with the image of a space battle ax, inspired by Japanese animation, of which Maximilian Büsser is a big fan), with four barrels ensuring a seven-day power reserve.

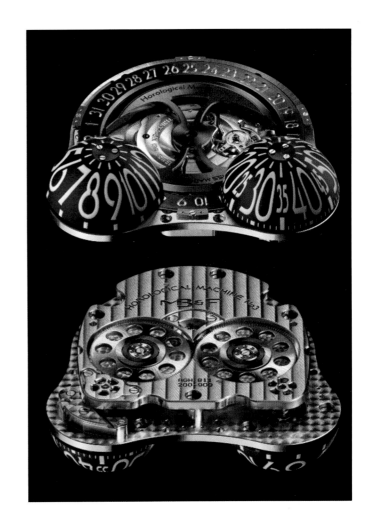

The other Horological Machine models repeat the characteristic dual-timer arrangement, adopting different complications and an imaginative aesthetic, distinctive for its unusual three-dimensionality, considered one of the MB&F trademark features. The LM1 (Legacy Machine N°1) boasts an equally unique personality, where the tradition of eighteenth- and nineteenth-century horologists is the inspiration for models with a classicizing imprint, interpreted with a touch of avant-garde technique.

Montblanc

Nicolas Rieussec HomeTime

Gold chronograph with dual time zone, dedicated to the inventor of the timing device on the short time intervals dial, 2012.

From writing instruments to time machines: Montblanc transfers its obsessive attention to detail from the desk to the wrists of enthusiasts of innovative horology.

The start of Montblanc dates to 1906. In that year, the banker Alfred Nehemias and the Berlin engineer August Eberstein launched production of fountain pens in Hamburg, registering the Montblanc brand in 1910. The rounded white star on the pen cap became the company symbol, later gracing the wide range of product categories in which Montblanc excels, thanks to its dedication to maintaining the highest quality standards in all of the areas of its activity. In the 1980s, the company made its debut in horology, but its timepiece division began a process of complete renovation in 1997, four years after the brand was acquired by the Vendôme group (which later became Richemont). The brand's signature collections include the Star and TimeWalker lines. In 2007, Montblanc united with Minerva, an illustrious Swiss manufacture specialized in mechanical chronometry, in the Montblanc production area. The Institut Minerva de Recherche en Haute Horlogerie is the cutting

Villeret 1858
Single-button chronograph in gold, manual-winding with dual tachymetric scale.

Time Walker
Self-winding chronograph with twenty-four hour and second time zone indication.

edge of the Montblanc horology division and developed the brand's first in-house movement, Caliber MB R100, which was used in the Nicolas Rieussec, a model dedicated to the inventor of the chronograph and distinctive for its unique distribution of chronographic functions on the dial. In 2010, the Metamorphosis was unveiled, a stunning design that can pass from one function to another through the perfectly synchronized shifting of elements on the dial. This model was followed by the Montblanc TimeWriter II Chronographe Bi-Frequence 1000, which can display even just one one-thousandth of a second.

Time Writer II Chronographe
White gold watch with manual-winding Minerva movement, limited series of 36 pieces, 2011.

A historic Swiss watch brand, which has registered more than one hundred patents in over a century, all distinctive for their technical and design excellence: the Polyplan and the Movado Museum are true masterpieces of style.

Movado

chilles Ditesheim, a young, talented horologist, founded Movado in La Chaux-de-Fonds in 1881. Given the fierce competition at the time, Ditesheim decided from the start to focus on production of high-quality watches with original designs. The name "Movado" (which means "always in motion" in Esperanto) was used for the first time in 1905, when a model produced in the Ditesheim atelier won the gold medal at the Liège Exposition. Seven years later, in 1912, the first Movado masterpiece was unveiled: the Polyplan. Its movement was articulated on three levels, an acrobatic design that made it possible to create a case with the winding crown at twelve o'clock and an elongated, anatomically curved shape, resulting in an object easily worn on the wrist.

A Movado advertisement from the 1950s.

uring World War I, the house produced "the soldier's watch", with a double case that protected the dial with slender but robust metal filigree. Designed for life in the trenches, the model was also popular among non-military customers. 1926 was the year of the Ermeto, a travel clock with a sliding case that wound the movement when opened and closed. The Ermeto was used in the 1930s by the Swiss aviator August Piccard during his flights. During this period, Movado became a staggering success, thanks to a series of timepieces inspired by the pure lines of modern architecture, including the Curviplan, an elegant watch with a curved bracelet, and the Chronographe.

Opposite
Polyplan

Pair of manual-winding watches with elongated steel cases and the crown at twelve o'clock, circa 1910.

Polyplan

Manual-winding watch with a rectangular steel case, crown at twelve o'clock, 1915.

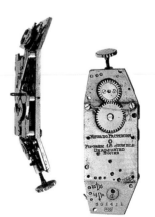

Caliber 400

The Polyplan manual-winding caliber; distinctive for the arrangement of the mechanism's elements on three distinct levels.

In 1947, the Movado introduced what would become its signature model, the Museum. Created by the American designer Nathan George Horwitt, it was tied to the aesthetic principles of the Bauhaus movement, which was led by Walter Gropius and promoted the idea of pure, practical production. The Museum watch is distinctive for its extreme simplicity: a round case dominated by a completely black dial with a single gold dot at twelve o'clock representing the sun. The model was dazzlingly received thanks to the extreme simplicity and refinement of its design. In the early 1950s, it was added to the permanent collection of the Museum

Museum
Electronic quartz watch, with a yellow gold case, reissue of a model designed by Nathan George Horwitt at the end of the 1940s, circa 1990.

Military
Manual-winding watch with a silver case and a filigree protective cover, produced for World War I soldiers, 1914. Below, the watch movement.

of Modern Art (MoMA) in New York. In the 1970s and 80s, Movado linked its name to celebrities in the worlds of sports, music and art. In keeping with this strategy, in 1987, Andy Warhol designed the Times/5 for Movado, comprising five rectangular watchcases that together also served as the bracelet. The distinctive feature of this watch was the use of a different dial for each case, decorated with black and white photos of New York taken by Warhol himself. Other illustrious figures who contributed to Movado creations include Yaacov Agam, a pioneer of kinetic art, and Max Bill, an exponent of the systematic and logic-based art movement known as "concrete art". All exceptional pieces, united in the extreme originality of their designs and limited production.

Chronograph
Manual-winding watch with a platinum case, antimagnetic, mobile horns, 1938.

Times/5
Five separate but connected watches, designed by Andy Warhol, circa 1980.

Military
Manual-winding chronograph with a steel case and minute counters at three o'clock, circa 1940.

Pilot
Manual-winding watch, with a steel case and a bezel that can be adjusted using the crown at two o'clock.

Luminor Panerai

Manual-winding watch with eight-day power reserve and a steel
case; prototype commissioned by the Egyptian Navy, 1956.
Left, the mechanical depth gage, circa 1940.
Below, the underwater wrist compass, circa 1940.

Officine Panerai inherited a wealth of technical solutions from more than a century of experimentation in the area of high technology for men in uniform. And started applying them to wristwatches in 1938.

Officine Panerai

The origins of Officine Panerai are found in Florence, where Giovanni Panerai opened the first timepiece shop on the Ponte alle Grazie in 1860, later moving the shop to the Palazzo Archiverscovile in Piazza San Giovanni. A reference point in Tuscany and the local partner of the most prestigious foreign houses, including Rolex, Longines, and Vacheron Constantin, the shop, which became a well-organized business under the leadership of Guido Panerai, started producing optical and high precision instruments, becoming a supplier

Luminor 1950

Manual-winding watch with a large (47 millimeter) steel case, patented crown protector, limited edition of 1950 pieces, 2002.

for the Italian Defense Ministry and the Royal Italian Navy. Officine Panerai produced self-illuminating devices for shooting at night, underwater compasses and depth gages for the commandos and shock troops of the Italian Gamma Group, the heroes of legendary feats during World War II on board Italian SLCs (slow running torpedoes called "maiali" or "pigs" in Italian). It was a short step from technical instruments to watches: robustness, impermeability and optimal legibility in all conditions were the requisites.

The commandos of the Gruppo Gamma of the Italian Navy, on board "maiali" torpedoes.

After a period of experimentation, resulting in a the creation of a few prototypes in 1936, the company began producing a small series of watches in 1938 featuring a large (47 millimeters in diameter) cushion-shaped case, wire horns, a screw-down back and crown and a Rolex movement. The most unusual aspect of the model was its sandwich dial, comprising

Luminor

Manual-winding watch with eight-day Angelus mechanism, steel case, small seconds at nine o'clock, crown-protecting bridge, circa 1950.

"Egyptian" Radiomir
Watch produced for the Egyptian Navy, with a large steel case, 1956.

Radiomir
Manual-winding watch with a Rolex movement, steel case and screw-down crown, baton indices, Arabic and Roman numerals, 1938.

Titanium Panerai
Self-winding watch with a titanium case waterproof up to 1,000 meters, prototype that never entered into production, circa 1980.

On this and the opposite page, a few studies of the bezel, crown-protecting bridge and dial of Panerai watches currently being produced.

a black upper plate with perforated hour markers and Arab numerals (at three, six, nine and twelve o'clock) and a bottom plate with numerals in relief and a layer of Radiomir, a luminescent substance made out of zinc sulfur, radium bromide (from which the name "Radiomir" was derived) and mesothorium.

The evolution of Officine Panerai watches involved the modification of their wire horns, replaced by fixed horns, and a major new invention: the crown-protecting bridge, patented by Panerai in 1956, where the crown is protected by a special lever bridge secured with screws, such that the time indications could be regulated by simply lifting this lever to operate the crown. The manual-winding Rolex Caliber was joined by the Angelus Caliber, which was also manual-winding but with an eight-day power reserve, so it did not need to be wound as often (models with the Angelus Caliber were distinguished from those with the Rolex Caliber by the former's aesthetically unusual placement of small seconds at nine o'clock); Radiomir, a highly radioactive and therefore dangerous material, was replaced by Luminor, a tritium-based material that canceled out all risk while providing a high degree of luminosity to the dial.

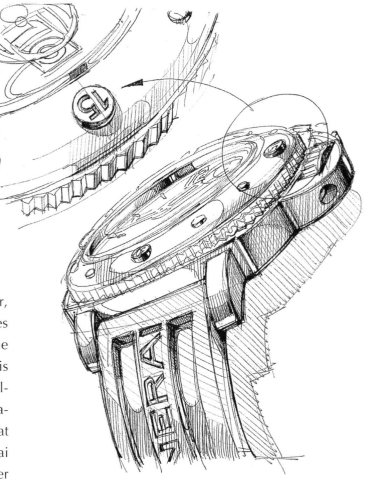

Among the models with a military character, distinguished for their high-impact shapes and aesthetics and over-sized cases, the design created for the Egyptian Navy in 1956 is of special interest, with a case measuring 66 millimeters in diameter and a rotating bezel for measuring immersion times and markers positioned at five-minute intervals. Experimentation led Panerai to develop a design in 1980 that, although it never made it past the prototype stage, was remarkable for its titanium case water-resistant up to 1,000 meters and solution for lighting the dial, based on an Officine Panerai patent from 1914 and involving little glass tubes filled with tritium and attached to the dial (acting as baton indices). In the 1990s, the company decided to change its target market, shifting from models designed for military use to a collection dedicated to connoisseurs of exceptionally well-made, robust mechanical timepieces. In 1993, this strategy led to the reissue of the Luminor and the Mare Nostrum, a chronograph with two timers and "pump" style buttons, three of which had been made in 1943, never entering into full production. In 1996, the actor Sylvester Stallone commissioned a special series of customized pieces bearing the inscription Slytech. In 1997, Officine Panerai was acquired by the Vendôme Group, which later became the Richemont Group. The international re-launching of Panerai followed a careful market-

ing strategy and involved a scrupulous process of product rationalization, focused on a style aimed to intrigue and seduce connoisseurs.

Radiomir 47 mm

Manual-winding watch with a vintage Rolex mechanism, platinum case, limited series of 60 pieces, 1997. Left, the mechanism seen from the back.

Luminor Marina Left-Handed
Manual-winding watch with a steel case and a crown-protecting bridge on the left, circa 2000.

Luminor Chrono
Self-winding chronograph with a steel case, circa 2000.

Luminor Tantalium
Manual-winding watch with a tantalum case, limited series of 300 pieces, 2003.

Radiomir Chrono
Manual-winding chronograph with a steel case and a vintage Valijoux movement, limited series of 230 pieces, 2003.

The names Radiomir and Luminor, which conjure up the house's twentieth-century quest for a truly effective luminescent material, also denote, in the company's new path, the two collections in Panerai's product catalog. Radiomir follows the watch layout from 1938, with a few exemplars of high value to collectors, like the Radiomir with a platinum case measuring 47 millimeters in diameter and a vintage Rolex movement, in a limited edition of sixty pieces (produced in 1997). At first produced only in special editions, the Radiomir case hosted a tourbillon and numerous chronograph versions, simple and rattrapante, with rare and precious vintage mechanisms.

Since 2004, this line has included models for everyday use, generally made of steel and equipped with mechanically simpler calibers. Examples include the Radiomir 45 mm Black Seal, the Radiomir 8 Days and the Radiomir GMT. Luminor is instead a collection based on the company's patented crown-protecting bridge, which guarantees impermeability, and featuring a robust case, in most models water resistant up to 300 meters, but going all the way up to 2,500 meters in the Luminor Submersible 2500M. Practical models, adhering to a construction logic focused on maximum robustness, the Luminor line pairs "time only" movements (self-winding or manual-winding) with basic complications like chronograph, GMT and power reserve.

Black Seal Compass

Compass with a titanium
and steel case, reissue
of a 1950s model,
limited series of
300 pieces, 2004.

Portable testing device
for timing torpedoes,
produced for Italian
Navy Officers,
circa 1940.

The brand's technical evolution surged ahead, and in 2005 Officine Panerai presented its first entirely in-house movement, Caliber P.2002. Manual-winding with eight-day power reserve, inspired by the Angelus mechanisms of the by then distant past, it introduced an intriguing way of displaying the power reserve, using a horizontally-sliding triangular indicator. In 2006, Panerai, by virtue of its patently Italian creativity, was selected to design Ferrari's high-end timepiece line, launching a partnership that lasted for five years and resulted in two primary collections, Granturismo and Scuderia. But manufacturing is the main focus of the Florentine company, which has created a prolific range of calibers, standing out among which is the P.2005, featuring dual time zone enhanced by a mobile tourbillon cage. Scientific experimentation has led Officine Panerai to cross new frontiers, like its creation of the Jupiterium, a complex planetarium-clock honoring the four-hundredth anniversary of the observations carried out by Galileo Galilei using an astronomical telescope, while the company's interest in using new materials has led to the production, in a limited series of 1,000 pieces, of the Luminor Submersible 1950 3 Days Automatic Bronzo 47MM, with a satin-finish case and dark green dial.

Luminor Submersible 1950 3 Days
Self-winding mechanism with three-day power reserve and a satin-finish bronze case, limited series of 1,000 pieces.

Luminor 1950 8 Days

Manual-winding mechanism with 192-hour power reserve and a satin-finish steel case, limited series of 150 pieces.

Radiomir 1936

Manual-winding mechanism with 56-hour power reserve and a steel case with a Plexiglas crystal, limited series of 1936 pieces.

The Egyptian

Maels, eight-day power reserve and a titanium case, nual-winding mechanical watch with three barr limited series of 500 pieces.

Radiomir 1940 Special Edition

Manual-winding mechanical watch with a Minerva movement and a red gold case with a Plexiglas crystal, limited series of 100 pieces.

The star of space missions and sea adventures, this Swiss house is famed for its mechanical reliability and brilliance at taking on time with a combination of tradition and the avant-garde. And also for being the first watch company to go to the Moon.

Omega

F ounded in 1848 by Louis Brandt in La Chaux-de-Fonds, the company moved to Bienne at the end of the nineteenth century, by which time it already had 600 employees and produced around 100,000 timepiece mechanisms each year (the reference year for this data is 1889). The name "Omega", however, dates to 1894, and is linked to the Omega 19-ligne caliber for pocket watches, distinctive for the complete interchangeability of its components. This mechanism was positively received by the public and became a strong part of the company's identity, which then took the name "Omega" in 1903.

A ttentive to new market trends, Omega made an early debut in the world of wristwatches: its first exemplars were rudimentary attempts, with cases poorly adapted for wearing on the wrist, generally featuring jointed horns and shapes far removed from those known today. Already in the 1930s, Omega was putting itself to the test, taking on the biggest challenges posed by technological progress. One of the biggest technical priorities was to develop

An astronaut during a space mission.

Speedmaster

Manual-winding chronograph with a steel case and bracelet and an arrow-shaped hour hand, 1957.

Opposite
Speedmaster

Manual-winding chronograph with a steel case and bracelet, the first and only watch to have been worn on the Moon, circa 1990.

Speedmaster

Back of watch shown on the opposite page, with engravings celebrating the watch's space adventure.

a waterproof watch, to resolve frequent problems with wristwatch use, and Omega's entry in this arena was the Marine, featuring a "double case" with an internal case housing the mechanism and an external, hermetically-sealed case. Experimentation with the Marine was followed by the Seamaster, which was presented in a range of variants and would become one of the stars of Omega's permanent collection.

1932 brought another important milestone to the house, with Omega selected as the Official Timekeeper for the Olympic Games in Los Angeles, supplying equipment and instruments for measuring the athletes' performance and launching a years-long collaboration in search of accuracy to one one-thousandth of a second. Omega also dedicated itself to the achievement of high mechanical and technical quality, distinguished by increasingly accurate precision, as evidenced by the numerous chronometry competition prizes awarded to the company by observatories. During World War II, Omega set itself apart for the supply of

watches designed for the military, characterized by robustness and reliability and later adapted for civilian use, as in the case of the brand's antimagnetic watches, like the Railmaster, with case or mechanism components that made it possible survive magnetic fields of significant intensity unharmed. Structural improvements were accompanied by aesthetic research, expressed in the understated, elegant lines typical of the 1950s and 60s, like the Constellation collection, unveiled in 1952 and a consistently able interpreter of Omega's aesthetic taste over the years. Another sales champion was the Cosmic, with a slender movement enhanced by the simplicity of the elements of the case, and indicators for the complete calendar laid out with beautiful graphic harmony. The Omega designers dedicated themselves to creating a range of product lines inspired by the strong economy (those were boom years in Europe and America) and, most of all, followed the early indications offering by marketing, a discipline that was just catching on and establishing itself during that period, focused on studying consumer trends: the "Elle e Lui"

Seamaster

Self-winding chronograph with a steel case, circa 1948. Left, the chronometer version, visually distinguished from the standard model by small seconds at six o'clock.

Speedmaster

Manual-winding chronograph with a steel case and a Velcro strap so that it could be worn over spacesuits, as described on its registration form.

Omega 19 linee

The pocket watch caliber that gave the manufacture its name.

GRAVÉ D'APRÈS PHOTOGRAPHIE

OMEGA

Vue de l'usine de la maison Louis Brandt et frère à Bienne.

Louis Brandt 13 linee

Manual-winding watch with minute repeater and a yellow gold case, 1892. Its origin in the pocket watch is clear from the structure of the case.

Seamaster 600 Ploprof

Self-winding watch with a steel case and bracelet, waterproof up to 600 meters, 1970.

Seamaster

Self-winding watch with a steel case and bracelet, waterproof up to 300 meters.

Seamaster Chrono Diver

Self-winding chronograph with a steel case and bracelet, waterproof up to 300 meters.

Jacques Mayol, one of the world's most famous divers, wearing an Omega Seamaster 120 Quartz, 1981.

Seamaster 120

Self-winding watch with a steel case, 1966.

series, in which a single model was produced in two distinct versions, one for women and one for men, is a clear example of Omega's ability to respond to market demand. Also of noteworthy aesthetic quality were the pieces designed for Omega by Gilbert Albert and Luigi Vignando, renowned jewelry designers whose models for the manufacture led to its winning prestigious awards at the Diamond International Awards, the Prix de la Ville de Genève and the Golden Rose of Baden–Baden.

In the 1970s, the struggle for technological supremacy in horology favored and inspired innovation. Omega was an active participant in the quartz revolution, introducing what would become two cornerstones of wrist electronics: the 1974 Constellation Megaquartz Marine Chronometer, then and now the most precise wristwatch in the world due to its 2,359,296 Hz frequency, seventy-two times greater than a that of a quartz watch produced today (a frequency of 32.768 Hz is the normal standard), and the 1976 Chrono-Quartz, the first timepiece with a dual system using both analog and digital display, the former for time and the latter for chronograph functions. Structural innovation was represented by the Seamaster 600 PloProf, with an over-sized case that could withstand high pressure levels: thanks to its extreme robustness, it was used during scientific explorations of the sea floor in the Gulf of Lion and the Gulf of Ajaccio. The most fascinating technical innovation used by Omega, acquired by the Swatch Group, is the Co-Axial escapement, a device that optimizes the watch movement's chronometric performance and was designed by the brilliant twentieth-century watchmaker, George Daniels.

Marine
Manual-winding watch with a double steel case that guarantees excellent watertightness, circa 1930.

Advertising poster designed for the 1932 Olympic Games in Los Angeles.

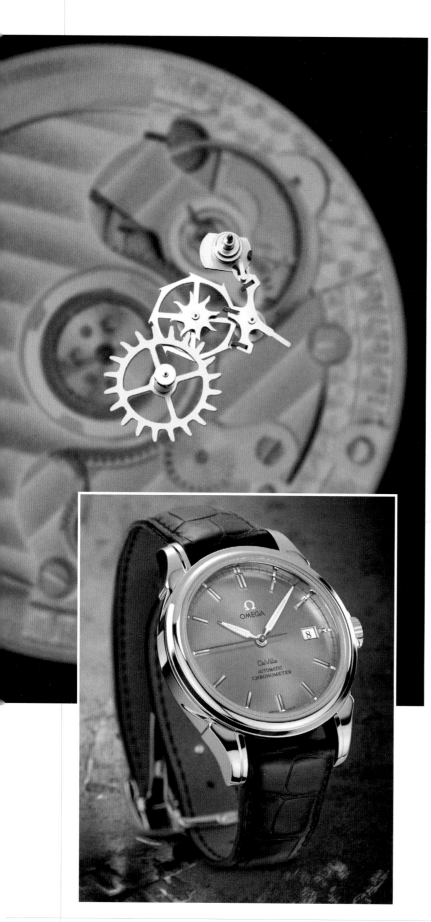

Omega's fundamental achievement, however, is tied to the conquest of the Moon: in July 1969, the astronauts of the Apollo XI mission wore the Speedmaster, a manual-winding chronograph selected by the NASA engineers following rigorous testing to assist the crew during space exploration. After the lunar surface adventure, the Omega Speedmaster Professional became known as the "Moon Watch" and opened the path for its successor, the 1998 Speedmaster Professional X-33, a multifunction quartz model destined for future space missions, perhaps even accompanying astronauts on Mars.

Co-Axial

Self-winding watch with a steel case and Co-Axial escapement, 2000. Above, the Co-Axial escapement, invented by the English watchmaker George Daniels and used in many of Omega's latest mechanisms.

Megaquartz 2400

Electronic quartz watch, gold and steel case, runs at a frequency of 2,359,296 Hz (traditional quartz watches run at 32,678 Hz). Thanks to its extreme precision, it was awarded a Marine Chronometer certificate in Neuchâtel in 1974.

Speedmaster X-33

Multifunction electronic quartz watch with a combined analog and digital display, 1998. It has been labeled the "Mars watch" for its chronometric and calculation potential.

Plodrof Co-Axial

Waterproof up to
1,200 meters with safety
crown and rotating bezel,
steel case, self-winding
movement, 2009.

Seamaster Aqua Terra Gmt

Watch with dual time zone
and date, steel case and
self-winding movement with
Co-Axial escapement.

De Ville Hour Vision

Certified chronometer
watch, steel case and
sapphire crystal, self-winding
movement with Co-Axial
escapement, 2007.

Spacemaster Z-33

Multifunction watch with
dual time zone, calendar
and chronograph,
titanium case and quartz
movement, 2012.

Often paired with world famous endorsers, chosen from among top athletes and the most famous Hollywood stars, Omega is always true to its vocation for celebrating the tradition of classic horology with original aesthetic solutions. The Hour Vision was designed to elevate observation of the mechanism from all angles through the use of sapphire glass not only on the back and but also on the sides of the case, where the manufacturing prestige of the mechanism is usually exalted through the use of noble metals for the fabrication of certain components. The use of innovative materials has become a must for Omega, as in the Ladymatic, made exclusively for women, which pairs steel, gold and diamonds with a dynamic, creative use of ceramic. The silicon spring, a component that markedly improves the regularity and chronometric performance of its watches, is another feature expressive of Omega's exceptional technological progress in recent years.

Seamaster Planet Ocean

Chronograph waterproof up to 600 meters with helium valve, titanium case and self-winding Co-Axial movement, 2011.

Parmigiani

M ichel Parmigiani, a master horologist with a talent for creating true masterpieces, opened his business in 1975, specializing in producing complicated calibers and restoring old and rare watches. Among the pieces he returned to their former splendor were a few exemplars restored for the Sandoz Family Foundation, which later decided to financially back Parmigiani's official entry into the horology field, celebrated in 1994 with the brand Parmigiani Fleurier. Production is limited to just a

A Swiss manufacture that rests the bases
for its success on the creativity of its founder,
Michel Parmigiani, who produces exclusive,
sometimes unique, pieces for his customers,
who can request any kind of decorative
or functional customization.

few hundred pieces per year, its target is the highest end of the market and its movements are made in-house. The Toric line, with round classic cases, was complemented by the Ionica collection, with tonneau-shaped cases and eight-day power reserve. In 1999, the Basica was unveiled, followed by a perpetual calendar with a retrograde calendar hand and a manual-winding rattrapante chronograph.

Parmigiani continued his technical experimentation, creating a new self-winding movement, a Westminster minute repeater with GMT and another unique piece, the Minute Repeater with perpetual calendar and tourbillon, followed in 2004 by a tourbillion with a cage rotation of thirty seconds instead of one minute. But the most stunning exemplar, developed in collaboration with Bugatti, is Parmigiani's manual-winding wristwatch with ten-day power reserve and a horizontally-oriented mechanism arranged on multiple plates aligned over the length of the case.

Toric Unique
Tourbillon with minute repeater and perpetual calendar; one of a kind.

Toric
Self-winding chronograph with a gold case.

The house then signed an agreement with Hermès for the supply of fine straps, with the aim of further increasing the exclusivity of its timepieces. In 2003, the company underwent radical reorganization, resulting in a new business structure divided into four operational units, each with its own defined goals and tasks, which collaborate in the integrated development of Parmigiani watches and, upon request, the production of models for select haute horology houses.

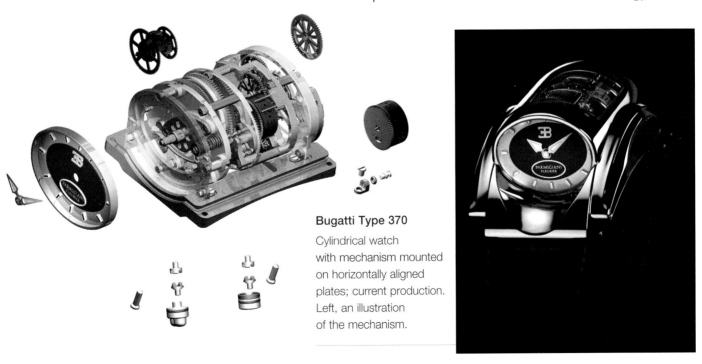

Bugatti Type 370
Cylindrical watch with mechanism mounted on horizontally aligned plates; current production. Left, an illustration of the mechanism.

Sky Moon Tourbillon

Tourbillon, minute repeater, perpetual calendar and celestial map (on the back): an absolute masterpiece with a yellow gold case, 2001.

A history defined by tradition, elegance and superior technics. Since 1939, Patek Philippe has represented the evolution of haute horology, producing models with a high emotional value that are preserved and passed down for generations.

Patek Philippe

The founding of Patek Philippe dates to 1839, when Count Antoine Norbert de Patek and François Czapek established Patek, Czapek & Cie; later, with the arrival of the Frenchman Jean Adrien Philippe (1845), the company name became Patek & Co. and, still later, Patek Philippe & Co. Jean Adrien Philippe applied his own mechanical expertise to the company's watch production, introducing, among other things, a manual winding system integrated with the setting of the time, thus making it unnecessary to use a key. The success of the first Patek Philippe models was based on the exceptional quality of the mechanisms and the designs' refined aesthetic taste: among the owners of these first pieces one finds Queen Victoria, who was won over by the beauty of a pocket watch decorated with enamel and precious stones. Other famous figures acquired Patek Philippe watches over the years, some from the house's traditional collections and others produced on commission, and the brand became a distinctive emblem of high society.

The Patek Philippe headquarters in an image from the 1930s.

Calatrava

Manual-winding watch with a yellow gold case, circa 1940.

Chronograph

Manual-winding watch with perpetual calendar and a yellow gold case, reference 1518, circa 1940.

The company achieved this status through a smart expansion strategy, distinguished already in its early years by targeted business agreements with such jewelers as Tiffany & Co. of New York and Gondolo & Labouriau of Rio de Janeiro. Patek Philippe's collaboration with Gondolo involved the creation of special pocket watch and wristwatch models with highly legible dials and gears made out of 9-carat gold. And the sales technique adopted by the Brazilian business in the early twentieth century, called the "Plano do Club Patek Philippe", was as curious as it was effective. In order to increase Patek Philippe sales, a committee of aficionados was established that fractioned the cost of the Patek Philippe model they wished to acquire into seventy-nine weekly payments. Periodic lottery draws made it possible for members to acquire their watches after as little as one week, with no further payments required: the winner of the draw would receive their watch, while the other members remained on the seventy-nine week payment plan for the receipt of their Patek Philippes.

In the 1910s and 20s, the house achieved the absolute highest levels of quality, especially in the area of pocket watches, with the Duke of Regla, which featured an exceptional system of musical chimes, and the pieces made for James Ward Packard and Henry Graves Junior, both businessmen with a passion for Patek Philippe watches. Technical advancement that would then also come to wristwatch models, the debut of which dates to 1868, with a women's diamond and gold model sold to the Hungarian Countess Koscowicz in 1876 and considered one of the world's first wristwatches. But it was not until the twentieth century that this new way of "wearing time" fully established itself at Patek Philippe: from models for women, with cases and bracelets

Print advertisement for the Ellipse d'Or, 1970s.

PATEK PHILIPPE

A nulle autre pareille

L'Ellipse d'Or Patek Philippe.
Exclusive, l'Ellipse d'Or est née de l'antique Règle d'Or. Unique, l'or bleu 18 carats des cadrans est une création de Patek Philippe. L'une et l'autre identifient des bijoux

entièrement travaillés à la main: les bijoux Patek Philippe.

Extraits de la collection Ellipse d'Or Patek Philippe: montres pour dame et homme, anneau de clés et boutons de manchettes.

9000 GENT **de Breuck & Willemot** TÉLÉPHONE (091) 25 78 30
JOAILLIERS-ORFÈVRES
FOURNISSEURS BREVETÉS DE LA COUR

Ellipse d'Or
Self-winding watch with a yellow gold case, circa 1980.

made of precious metals and enameled dials, to the first pieces derived from pocket watches, finally arriving at designs with proportions and mechanisms conceived according to "wrist logic".

Of special interest in this arena is a 1925 Perpetual Calendar with lunar phases now preserved in the Patek Philippe museum. Its yellow gold case has engraved, decorated horns and the back is attached with a hinge, with clear reference to pocket models. In 1932, the company debuted one of its most important wristwatches, the Calatrava. Its name was inspired by the Calatrava cross, a religious symbol previously used as the Patek Philippe logo and which had become the standard of the Swiss manufacture's models with a round case. The first Calatrava was the Ref 96 (each new Patek Philippe is assigned a special reference code, and these codes are cited from memory by the brand's passionate collectors). A manual-winding watch, it had a smooth bezel, which later came to be embellished with "clous de Paris" decoration, a motif that became part of the tradition of the house's rich catalog.

The round case of the Calatrava hosted a wide range of mechanisms, some manual-winding, others self-winding, and complications including the perpetual calendar and the chronograph. The dials, decorated with hands, hour markers and numerals of various kinds, were sometimes made of enamel, and the cases came in yellow, white and rose gold as well as platinum.

Rattrapante chronograph
Manual-winding watch with a yellow gold case and a black dial; one of a kind, 1952.

Chronograph
Manual-winding watch with a yellow gold case and black dial, reference 5070, 1998.

Decorated horns

Manual-winding watch with a non-circular white and yellow gold case, circa 1940.

he year 1932 marked a turning point for Patek Philippe, but not only for the unveiling of the Calatrava. In order to cope with the grave consequences of the stock market crash of 1929, which brought with it a worrying drop in sales, in 1932, the descendants of the founders ceded control of the company to the brothers Charles and Jean Stern, who ensured the house's continuity and financial stability. In addition to the Calatrava, a number of non-circular models were introduced, featuring rectangular, square and tonneau cases shapes, as well as lines echoing the movements. Maximum attention was paid to the purest mechanics, resulting in devices put into production only after rigorous experimentation in order to ensure absolute reliability. That is why the brand's first self-winding model was not unveiled until 1953, late in the game compared to the company's competitors, but the Patek Philippe models almost always have a gold rotor. The complicated watches are especially intriguing, and include chronographs, tourbillons and minute repeaters. After the first exemplars, developed from pocket watch models, the company's wristwatch designs were characterized by the consistent application of the most advanced technical refinements. Ref 130 is Patek

Reference 2554

Manual-winding watch with a non-circular yellow gold case, circa 1950.

Decorated horns

Manual-winding watch with a non-circular white and yellow gold case, circa 1930.

Reference 5100, 10 Days

Manual-winding watch with ten-day power reserve, rose gold case, limited edition of 1,500 pieces in yellow gold, 750 in rose gold, 450 in white gold and 300 in platinum, 2000.

PATEK PHILIPPE
GENEVE
WATCHMAKERS TO LADIES SINCE 1839

*Print advertisement
for the Nautilus, 1980s.*

Nautilus
Self-winding watch
with a steel case
and bracelet,
circa 1980.

Philippes' most successful family of chronographs, although the
house abandoned the fabrication of
simple chronographs in the 1950s (not
returning to the production of this type of watch until
1998), offering this complication only in combination
with others, like perpetual calendar.

Aquanaut
Self-winding
watch with a steel
case and natural
rubber strap.

Aquanaut
Self-winding watch
with a steel case
and bracelet.

The manufacture's most interesting specialties
include its World Time models, which feature
the names of the cities representing each time
zone on the bezel or an area of the dial. This complication was worked out by Louis Cottier, the talented
artisan who came up with a range of mechanical and

aesthetic solutions for some of the most interesting designs produced by Patek Philippe between 1937 and the 1960s, with different specificities, one or two crowns for regulating the cities and dials often embellished with cloisonné enamel. At Patek Philippe, technics are always in the foreground, as with the Gyromax balance wheel, patented in 1949, which permits precise regulation through tiny pegs arranged around the rim; the introduction of the annual calendar, with a mechanism that automatically calculates months lasting thirty or thirty one days (and so excepting February), and, in 2005, the adoption of silicon for the escapement wheel.

In the 1970s, Patek Philippe was dedicated to developing its first sport watch, the Nautilus, which was designed by Gérald Genta and featured a steel case and bracelet. Later updated with small complications (power reserve and analog date), the Nautilus paved the way for the Aquanaut, a model that represented a radical change from the rigid classicism of Patek Philippe, appreciated for its strong, aggressive look reinforced by a natural rubber strap. This sport aesthetic was also applied to women's models, always an area of focus for the house, with lines presenting reduced-scale versions of the men's models and, in 1999, a new entry: the Twenty~4, which juxtaposed steel and diamonds, creating a combination with a strong personality.

The period coinciding with the 150th anniversary of Patek Philippe's foundation, celebrated in 1989, was full of new developments, with models produced in extremely limited editions and that would never be offered again with the same characteristics, since the tools used to create them were afterwards

Perpetual Calendar Chronograph

Manual-winding watch with a yellow gold case and black dial, probably one of a kind, reference 2499, 1998.

Rattrapante Chronograph

Manual-winding watch with a yellow gold case, circa 1930.

Rattrapante Chronograph Perpetual Calendar

Manual-winding perpetual calendar watch with a gold case, 1955.

Print advertisement
for the Patek Philippe
Perpetual Calendar,
1950s.

Left
Calatrava

Manual-winding watch with
perpetual calendar, lunar phases
and a platinum case, 1939.

Right
Calatrava

Manual-winding watch with
complete calendar, lunar phases
and a platinum case, 1938.

destroyed. Included in this exclusive group were the Officier, with a case characterized by a hinged back, recalling the design of watches made for World War I officers, and the tonneau Jumping Hours, with the hour indicated in a little window on the dial at twelve o'clock. Standing out among them all was the Caliber 89, the most complicated watch ever made: the calendar, chronograph and chime functions were displayed on the two dials, which presented thirty-three indications overall. Here are a few numbers to better illustrate the Caliber 89: 9 years of research and development, 1,728 components, 126 of which are rubies, contained in a sumptuous case measuring 89 millimeters in diameter and 41 millimeters thick.

World Time

Manual-winding watch
with world time indication
and a platinum case,
probably one of a kind,
1939–1940.

Enamel Dial

Manual-winding watch
with a yellow gold
case and a cloisonné
dial, 1956.

World Time

Manual-winding watch
with double crown
world time indication, a
yellow gold case and a
cloisonné dial, 1955.

World Time Chronograph

Manual-winding chronograph
with world time indication
and a yellow gold case,
one of a kind, 1940.

In 2001, the company opened the Patek Philippe
museum to share and preserve the masterpieces created by the manufacture since its founding in 1839
as well as to display the wondrous devices produced
between the sixteenth and nineteenth centuries by the
world's great horologists. This museum offers a window
on best of the world of watches.

Minute Repeater

Self-winding watch
with a platinum case,
reference 5029,
limited series of
10 pieces, 1997.

Minute Repeater

Manual-winding
watch with a yellow
gold case, 1959.

Reference 5270

Manual-winding mechanical watch with chronograph, twenty-four hours and perpetual calendar with lunar phases, white gold case with interchangeable back in sapphire glass and white gold.

The third millennium has been technologically distinguished by two important chapters in the company's history: the establishment of Patek Philippe Advanced Research, which, starting in 2001, has worked with major research centers in Neuchâtel and Lausanne and, in 2011, the creation of the Patek Philippe chair at the Ecole Polytechnique Federale de Lausanne (EPFL). The Geneva house is deeply passionate about this initiative and, together with the EPFL, established it to reward impetus towards innovation by supporting research on new applications of microtechnology and nanotechnology in the horology sphere. The most important result of this research thus far is Sininvar, a silicon alloy used to produce the Pulsomax escapement and the Spiromax balance spring, both components designed by the Advanced Research division. The Patek Philippe Seal, a quality seal introduced in 2009, certifies the brand's commitment to the constant, continuous improvement of its watches, in accordance with strict quality standards for precision and maintenance.

Nautilus

Self-winding mechanical watch with patented annual calendar, twenty-four hours and lunar phases, waterproof case and steel bracelet.

Reference 5170

Manual-winding mechanical watch with a column wheel chronograph, gold case and bracelet and a back that reveals the movement.

World Time

Self-winding mechanical watch with twenty-four time zones indicated with their key city names, white gold case.

Reference 5140

Self-winding ultra-thin mechanical watch with twenty-four-hour indication, perpetual calendar with lunar phases and a platinum case.

While Patek Philippe's manufacturing activity is instead focused on the chronograph, especially in combination with calendar or minute repeater functions. After its presentation in 2005 of the world's thinnest rattrapante chronograph caliber, the next year the company introduced a chronograph with an annual calendar. 2009 was the year of the simple chronograph and, successively, the grand complications division was updated with new mechanisms pairing the perpetual calendar with the simple chronograph and, finally, the rattrapante chronograph.

An aristocratic vocation for luxury has led to some of haute horlogerie's most breathtaking masterpieces. Designed by Piaget, of course, a company that interprets timepieces through jewels, diamonds and absolute exquisiteness.

Piaget

12P

In-house self-winding movement, 1960.

"Always do better than necessary." This was the motto of Georges Edouard Piaget, the founder of the eponymous house, a motto that clearly and unambiguously expresses the vocation for perfection and fine taste that has always been the company's guide. The Piaget manufacture was founded in 1874 in La Côte-aux-Fées. Specialized in producing high-quality mechanisms, the company only began its activity as an independent brand in the 1940s, thanks to the leadership of Gérald Piaget, who launched a wide-ranging marketing strategy with the assistance of Valentin Piaget, a master horologist and director of the production division. They were a winning pair: Gérald promoted the brand abroad during his travels and found buyers for the Valentin's precious creations. In

1956, Valentin designed the Caliber 9P, an ultra-thin manual mechanism measuring just two millimeters thick, a record-setting achievement that had a major technical impact. In 1960, Piaget patented its self-winding Caliber 12P, which had a gold rotor and an overall thickness of no more than 2.3 millimeters. At the end of the 1950s, Yves Piaget, Gérald's son, joined the company and contributed to the development of the brand with unique pieces and jewelry watches that demonstrated the house's exceptional mechanical expertise and brilliance at "dressing" mechanisms with extraordinary creations.

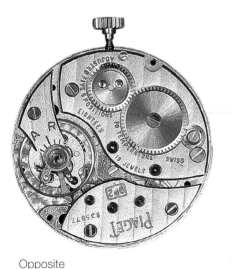

9P

In-house manufacture-winding movement, 1956.

Opposite
Yellow Gold

Ultra-thin watch with 9P mechanical movement, 1957.

White Gold

Ultra-thin watch with 9P mechanical movement, 1960.

Rectangular
Watch with arched case
in white gold,
9P mechanism, 1957.

Square
White gold watch with
"shantung" bezel and
dial, 9P mechanism,
1957.

Turquoise

Gold and precious
stone watch, 9P
mechanism, 1967.

Coral

Gold and
precious stone
bracelet watch,
9P mechanism, 1971.

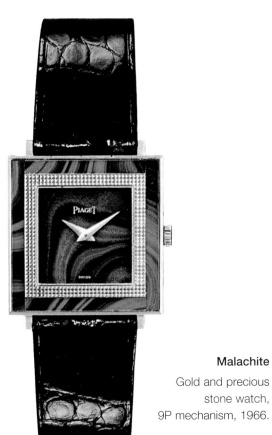

Malachite

Gold and precious
stone watch,
9P mechanism, 1966.

Turquoise and Lapis Lazuli

Gold and precious stone
conical bracelet watch,
9P mechanism, 1970.

In the 1970s, Piaget won acclaim for the stunning creativity of its watches for women and the winning combination of jewelry and technical innovation continued to be explored in the years to come, resulting in extraordinary models like the Phoebus of 1981, a gold and diamond design created for a wealthy Japanese customer. New calibers were also unveiled, including the ultra-thin manual 20P and the automatic 25P that derived from it, as well as the 1986 electronic quartz 30P with perpetual calendar. The Slave watch, designs with precious stone dials, the Polo and the classic Gouverneur all testify to Piaget's talent for expressing time with passion. Piaget was acquired by the Richemont Group in 1989, and while it preserved its own identity, based on limited numbers and the highest levels of quality, it was also able to draw on new resources for improving and increasing its production of mechanical watches. In the second half of the 1990s, Piaget produced an especially rich array of new creations: the Gouverneur line was expanded to include the Grande Sonnerie wristwatch, and the Caliber 500P and the Caliber 430P made their debuts in the areas of women's and non-circular models. Piaget also stepped into the sport horology arena for the first time, introducing the gold Polo Key Largo, which was waterproof up to 200 meters and followed by a chronograph version.

For the house's 125th anniversary, Piaget collaborated with Parmigiani and presented the Eight-Day Emperador, a jumping hours model with a classic style. In 2001, the house created an all-steel model for the first time in its history, the Upstream, with a satin-finish tonneau case and an unprecedented opening system, with the closure of the strap or bracelet attached directly to the case: to remove the watch from your wrist, all you needed to do was lift the bezel at twelve o'clock. One of the house's biggest successes was unquestionably the Tourbillon Emperador, introduced in 2002 and equipped with a manual caliber measuring 3.5 millimeters thick that confirmed Piaget's manufacturing genius. The brand's superiority was further reinforced by the Altiplano collection, featuring manual-winding and self-winding movements that demonstrate Piaget's aptitude for extreme mechanical slenderness.

Satin Finish
White and yellow gold watch, 9P mechanism, 1960.

Hammered
White and yellow gold watch, 9P mechanism, 1959.

Limelight Magic Hour

Jewelry watch in rose gold and diamond that can be rotated into three different positions on the white satin strap, ardillon buckle and white flinqué dial.

Technological experimentation experienced as an absolutely essential source of inspiration and carried out with the objective of using innovative materials for its cases and bracelets: Rado is synonymous with horology research and development.

Rado

The history of Rado is marked by two distinct moments. First, the founding of Schlup (named after the brothers who established the company) in 1917 in Lengnau. Schlup specialized in producing mechanisms and other watch parts for third parties. In 1954, Schlup & Co. perfected its internal production chain, creating complete watches and achieving mastery of valuable technical expertise. At that stage, the watches were not yet signed on the dial, since they were being sold to other businesses in the industry, but the company's desire to launch its own brand became reality in 1956. The brand's original name, "Exacto", was quickly replaced by "Rado" in 1957, opening the second chapter in the house's history, with the company producing a wide range of models, including the Green Horse, the Starliner Day-Night and the Captain Cook, all self-winding, a characteristic especially appreciated on the Asian markets.

Asian culture and its predilection for gold and brilliant materials motivated Paul Luthi, the chief executive of Rado at the time, to take an inspired strategic turn that led the Lengnau house to new success. This consumer group's constant requests to restore the original shine to the case and bracelet of their timepieces spurred Rado to finance the development of an alloy that could be used to produce a scratchproof watch. After a long series of metallurgical experiments, the DiaStar was unveiled in 1962, with a steel case treated with

Cerix

"Men's and women's" pair, electronic quartz, high-tech ceramic case.

Opposite
DiaStar 2

The first scratchproof self-winding mechanical watch, with a round case, 1962.

tungsten carbide and titanium carbide. This model won Rado international fame for the innovative materials used in its fabrication and its high-impact aesthetic, featuring a rounded, enveloping bezel with a shape partway between a tonneau and an oval. The evolution of the DiaStar continued over the years, with shapes and dials marked by imagination and color. The most fascinating experiments include the NCC (New Concept and Construction) models of the 1970s, with a special waterproof case made of metal and plastic.

From scratchproof metal, the company moved on to high-tech ceramic, unveiling the Integral in 1986, made of an aerospace material (used for the Space Shuttle's thermal shield), aluminum and zirconium oxide. This alloy requires special processing at high temperatures (up to 1,450 degrees Celsius) and involving pressure or injection procedures. A second process, called metalization, gives surfaces, sapphire glass included, the part shiny, part transparent tonality that is typical of Rado watches.

v10k

Electronic quartz chronograph, case in a material with a hardness equal to that of a diamond.

DiaStar 67 "Glissière"

Electronic quartz watch, dial with diamond hour markers, 1976.

eSenza

"Men's and women's" pair, electronic quartz, steel case.

Acquired by the Swatch Group, Rado continued its quest for new materials, with the aim of satisfying a customer base that privileges the innovative style of its creations and the brand's ability to offer traditional horological mechanics together with avant-garde aesthetic design. DiaStar and Integral were followed by other collections, all distinguished by the same common denominator, technological quality: Sintra, DiaMaster, Ovation and Esenza. In 2002, Rado unveiled the v10k, a model with a scratchproof, highly resistant case made with a material that has a Vickers hardness of 10,000, equal to that of a diamond (traditional watches have a Vickers hardness of about 200).

Sintra

"Men's and women's" pair, electronic quartz, high-tech ceramic case.

DiaStar

Self-winding watch with day of the week indicator and calendar, scratchproof metal case, 1972.

Richard Mille

The founder of the brand that bears his name, Richard Mille is the "Formula 1 of horology", a description that embraces two industries well known to Mille through his previous professional experience and personal passion, two industries that share the horology world's quest for precision and quality of execution: aeronautics and car racing.

RM 009 Felipe Massa

Manual-winding watch with Alusic case, skeleton mechanism, sapphire glass dial with white Arabic numerals, limited series of twenty-five pieces. Above, a view of the movement showing its structural lightness.

Horological esotericism, with all of its innovative content, technology and artful forms, is interpreted by Richard Mille in wristwatches that are like little laboratories for experimentation with new materials and avant-garde forms.

The first watch line produced by the house dates to 2001, and was characterized by strong, aggressive cases with a "Blade Runner" aesthetic, ergonomic shapes that enhanced the personality of the design, exposed studs and high-impact satin finishes. The materials used were the traditional gold and platinum, joined by titanium and, following the most recent discoveries in experimental metallurgy, special alloys like ALUSIC, a combination of aluminum, silicon and carbon that is extremely hard to work with but lightweight and robust. Richard Mille used this alloy for the Tourbillon Felipe Massa: weighing just thirty grams, this model was dedicated to the Formula 1 racing driver and produced in a limited series of just twenty-five pieces. It was an incredible record. The technical performance of Richard Mille mechanisms is also superb, with classic complications (first and foremost, tourbillon, but also chronograph and self-winding) reinterpreted with intriguing stylistic choices and fabricated with metals like titanium and aluminum-lithium, a corrosion-resistant alloy used in aeronautics with a density almost half that of titanium. Features enhanced by the total transparency of the dial and the stylized, geometrically stripped-down hands and indicators, like the numerals for the hours and the calendar, which recall those of the first digital watches of the 1970s.

RM 005

Self-winding watch with titanium bridges and plates, date indicator at seven o'clock, titanium case, sapphire glass dial.

RM 004

Manual-winding rattrapante chronograph with a rose gold case. Left, the watch mechanism seen from the back.

Roger Dubuis

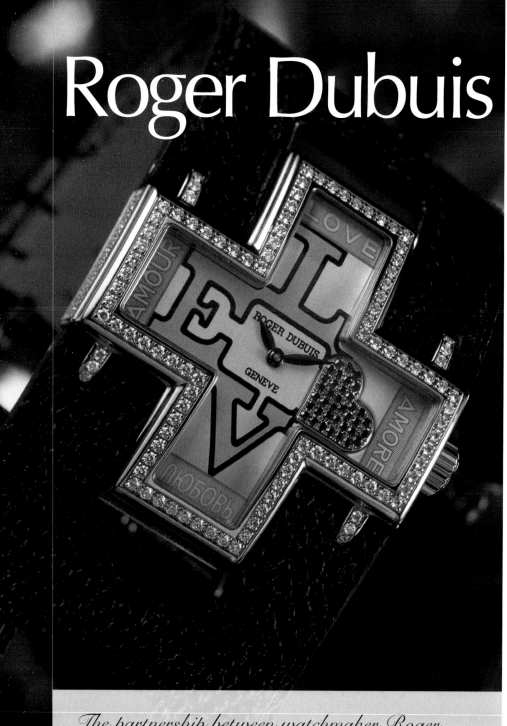

The partnership between watchmaker Roger Dubuis and entrepreneur Carlos Dias results in timepieces that wed style to technical beauty. Without losing sight of the traditions of the past, which inspire the house's creation of intriguing models with contemporary taste.

Left
FollowMe
Manual-winding watch
with a cross-shaped white gold
and diamond case and rubies
on the dial.

As has often happened in the history of horology, the founding of Roger Dubuis was the fruit of the joining of two souls: the exquisitely technical spirit of Dubuis, a master watchmaker who has been employed at the most renowned companies in the industry, and the business spirit, embodied by Carlos Dias, an ambitious entrepreneur who transformed the artisan's dream into a complex, well-organized company active in all of the world's primary markets. In 2008, Roger Dubuis was acquired by the Richemont group.

GoldenSquare
Manual-winding watch
with tourbillon, big date,
power reserve indicator
and a white gold case.

The Roger Dubuis manufacture was founded in Geneva in 1995. Its first models were unveiled the following year, with the introduction of two lines, Hommage, with a round case, and Sympathie, with an unprecedented square shape, with curved sides undulating toward the corners. Small series of twenty-eight pieces (the house's lucky number), above which some elements of the case or dial are varied, for an unprecedented level of exclusivity. The brand's watches are strictly mechanical and distinguished by the Poinçon de Genève, which certifies the high quality of the company's calibers and their place of production. Roger Dubuis reinterprets traditional watch complications through meticulously refined mechanisms and intriguing solutions (like using retrograde hands for various perpetual calendar indications or time information), while maintaining the technical quality of

Hommage
Self-winding watch with perpetual calendar, lunar phases and a rose gold case, Bulletin d'Observatoire certified, circa 1990.

Sympathie
Self-winding chronograph with a square "carrée cambrée" white gold case, Bulletin d'Observatoire certified, circa 2000.

MuchMore
Manual-winding watch with perpetual calendar and a white gold case.

MuchMore
Manual-winding single-button chronograph with a white gold case.

its pieces at the very highest levels. New collections for men have been added over the years, including MuchMore, GoldenSquare and SAW (Sport Activity Watch), featuring classic as well as ultra-sporty models, while the FollowMe line was developed for women, distinguished for the curious cross shape of the cases.

The watch most dreamed of, most desired, most copied and most envied
by the competition. Rolex is a company distinguished by big numbers, exceptional
quality and technological supremacy, and the producer of an incredible series of legendary
models: Prince, Submariner, GMT, Explorer, Day-Date and Daytona.

Rolex

R olex watches are considered the highest expression of functionality, paired with unmistakable design and characterized by superlative robustness and reliability. The company's origins date to the early twentieth century, when the German Hans Wilsdorf moved to London and founded, in 1905, Wilsdorf & Davis, a business specialized in the production and sale of watch cases. The house enjoyed satisfying sales numbers thanks to Wilsdorf's intuition, convinced that the wristwatch would be the modern replace-

Hans Wilsdorf, the founder of Rolex.

ment of the pocket watch. Wilsdorf's countless winning ideas included the introduction of the extensible bracelet, which made it possible to adapt the watch to any wrist. It was only a short step from success in the area of distribution to the creation of his own brand, and Rolex was founded on July 2, 1908 in La Chaux-de-Fonds, the site of a technical office that worked for Wilsdorf. Four year later, the brand was also registered in London. The company moved to Bienne in 1912, and then finally, seven years later, to Geneva, where Wilsdorf founded Manufacture des Montres Rolex SA.

Daytona

Self-winding chronograph with a white gold case and bracelet.

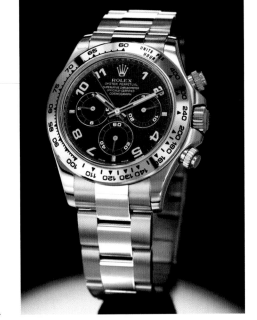

Opposite
Daytona "Paul Newman"

Manual-winding chronograph with a steel case and bracelet.

"Jean-Claude Killy" Chronograph

Manual-winding chronograph with calendar indication and a steel case, circa 1950.

A brilliant marketing man (and clearly ahead of his time, at least in the world of horology), Hans Wilsdorf worked in close contact with dealers and, in order to establish the Rolex brand, followed a few guidelines that proved to be a big success, so much so that they are still part of the industry's basic strategy today: a sustained advertising campaign, obsessive attention to the chronometric performance of the watches produced and mental openness to innovations that could provide a true competitive advantage over other houses.

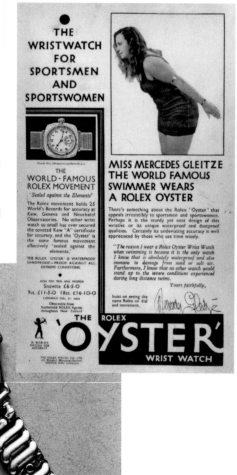

Print advertisement from the 1930s celebrating Gleitze's 1926 triumph.

Oyster

Manual-winding watch with a steel case and bracelet, worn by the swimmer Mercedes Gleitze during her swim across the English Channel in 1926.

In the area of precision, in 1914, the Kew Observatory in England awarded a class "A" certificate to a Rolex 11 ligne mechanism (about 25 millimeters in diameter). This was the first "chronometer certificate" awarded to a wristwatch by a chronometric observatory, a special division of an astronomic observatory where, until 1967, the accuracy of timepieces was assessed through rigorous testing carried out in different positions and at different temperatures (in Italy, this service was provided by the Brera Observatory in Milan). Thus began the "race to chronometry" and Rolex has been dedicated ever since to fabricating, in the vast majority of cases, movements qualified to receive the Official Chronometer Certificate.

But the evolution of Rolex horology involved two important innovations, each revolutionary because they completely upended the idea of fragility and unreliability that was still holding back the wrist models. One of the biggest problems concerned the impermeability of the case, which needed to keep the mechanism safe from stress, shocks, moisture and dust. The impermeable case had the task of protecting the movement from such intruders, the sworn enemies of gears, bridges and plates. And the numerous attempts to develop one in the 1920s were beat out by Rolex in 1926 with the introduction of a screw-down winding crown and, on October 18 of the same year, a patent for the Oyster case, the back of which (also screwed down and sealed with special gaskets) functioned like an extremely solid, hermetically sealed "oyster". This innovation was stunningly illustrated on October 21, 1927 by the English swimmer Mercedes Gleitze, who swam across the English Channel with a Rolex Oyster on her wrist. After more than fifteen hours of prolonged strenuous effort, the young swimmer happily showed off the wristwatch, which had arrived in England in perfect working order. Wilsdorf grasped the publicity potential of the event and spread the news all over the world: the image, published on the front page of the Daily Mail, can be considered one of the first business communication initiatives in the history of horology, and Rolex continued to implement this strategy over the years through its participation in prestigious sailing, golf and tennis sporting events.

Continuing its focus on improving wristwatch functionality, Rolex stunned the watch world in 1931 with a patent for a new invention: the Perpetual, a self-winding device with a central two-way rotor that not only effectively resolved the age-old problem of daily winding but also made it possible to avoid frequent use of the crown, which was needed only for regulating the watch, making the case less vulnerable and as a consequence also optimizing its hermetic seal. The Rolex Oyster and Perpetual became synonymous with impermeability and self-winding, marking a fundamental chapter in wristwatch history. Designs with classic shapes, including the first Rolex Tonneau and the Prince models, which had a rectangular, arched case and a dial with continuous seconds displayed in an area separate from the hour and minute indicators, were joined by the Oyster Perpetual Chronometer models, available in a range of variants and distinguished for a more modern look, like the so-called "Bubbleback" (called the "Little Egg" in Italian). Starting in the 1930s, the brand began unveiling manual-winding marine chronometers, standing out among which was the Oyster Chronograph Antimagnetic, with a case designed to resist magnetic interference. Rolex production after the war turned toward the self-winding movement, with the unveiling of the Oyster Perpetual Date-Just in 1945, a model distinguished for its unique style: a tonneau-shaped case, perfectly round

Oyster

Manual-wind watch with a yellow gold octagonal case, circa 1920.

Prince Brancard

Manual-winding watch with a white and yellow gold case, circa 1930.

Single-Button Chronograph

Manual-winding chronograph with a yellow gold case and a black dial, circa 1935.

The Oyster Case.
In case.

It takes us over a year to make a Rolex.

A good deal of this time is spent on performing the 162 separate operations it takes to turn a solid block of hardened stainless steel, or gold, into a virtually indestructible Rolex Oyster case.

We think it's time well spent. The men who wrote us the following letters obviously do, too.

From a Canadian deep-sea fisherman:

"The watch went down with the boat at 35 fathoms. The boat was submerged for 22 days.

"When the boat was raised I was there and went aboard to look for my watch. The watch was on the galley floor amongst mud, weeds, etc. I took it on the barge that raised the boat and washed it off, upon shaking the watch it commenced to go and was none the worse for the length of time it had been under. I continued to wear the watch without taking it to a jeweller."

From a British Admiralty civilian diver:

"As a final trial, the watch was lowered on the end of a steel wire to a depth of 400 feet, double the maximum depth to which it was possible to dive with independent compressed-air equipment. After an hour of this test no water had infiltrated into the watch."

From an underwater photographer in New Guinea:

"... My Rolex was put to an extremely hard test day after day for over three years. It was with me on countless dives (up to 100 feet), exposed for hours to sea water by shell collecting, hot showers, continuous contact with developer, stop bath, acid fixer in a dark room (including an accidental 9 hours in hypo), months in tropical rain forest on Sepik river. It stood up to a thousand knocks, abused to the limit, but remained sound."

Pictured:
The Rolex Oyster Datejust in steel, $255. Also available in steel/gold and 18 kt. gold.

From the leader of a Welsh Himalayan expedition:

"During the six and a half months spent away from the U.K. we experienced the widest possible range of temperature and humidity; the highest temperature being 117 deg. F. in the shade in Afghanistan to 34 deg. of frost at the top of the 19,000-ft. Urai Lagna pass near the Nepal-Tibet border when Harrop and I were returning from two months' imprisonment at the hands of the Chinese Communists.

"Our first check on the time broadcast by Radio Delhi in early January proved that both Harrop's Rolex and mine were within seconds of the correct time after five months away from civilisation."

(We would understand if you found these accounts difficult to believe. If you wish, we will send you a notary certified facsimile of any of the original letters from which these extracts are taken.)

There's really little else we can add.

Except to say that the Perpetual movement which the Oyster case protects is so accurate that it has been awarded the title of "chronometer" by one of the Official Swiss Institutes for Chronometer Tests.

And that letters like these make us feel more than ever justified in saying that each Rolex earns the recognition it enjoys.

Each Rolex earns the recognition it enjoys. You know the feeling.

ROLEX

American Rolex Watch Corporation 580 Fifth Avenue, New York, N.Y. 10036 Also available in Canada. Write for free color catalog.

Print advertisement for the Oyster case, 1950s.

Opposite
Datejust
Self-winding watch with a platinum case.

dial and a calendar at three o'clock. It was a timeless aesthetic, and remained unchanged over the years. The Oyster case then hosted chronograph mechanisms and complete calendars with lunar phases, while 1956 saw the debut of the Day-Date, the first self-winding wristwatch to indicate the date and the day of the week. Another line, the Cellini collection, was instead dedicated to more traditional models with manual-winding mechanisms (although in the 1970s, quartz movements started to be used as well).

In the 1950s, Rolex introduced a new way of thinking about horology, presenting a series of models, the Professionals, that entered the collective imag-

Oysterquartz Datejust
Electronic quartz watch with a steel case and white gold bezel, circa 1990.

Day-Date
Self-winding watch with date and day of the week indication and a platinum case and bracelet, circa 1980.

Datejust
Pair of watches, one for men, one for women, self-winding, steel and gold case.

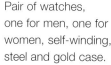

GMT

Self-winding watch
with dual time
zone indication
and a steel case
and bracelet,
circa 1980.

**Explorer II
"Steve McQueen"**

Self-winding watch with
dual time zone indication
and a steel case
and bracelet,
circa 1980.

Sea-Dweller

Self-winding watch
with a steel case
and bracelet,
waterproof up
to 610 meters,
circa 1970.

Submariner

Self-winding watch
with a steel case
and bracelet,
waterproof up
to 300 meters,
circa 1970.

ination of every aficionado. The first on the list was
the Submariner of 1953, which featured a simple
black dial that could be read in all light conditions,
a rotating bezel for calculating immersion times and
an Oyster case and extremely resistant Plexiglas crystal that ensured watertightness up to a depth of 200
meters. This model underwent numerous evolutions,
including increases to the size of the crown and the
addition of protective steel buffers. In 1986, a version with sapphire glass was introduced, which was
waterproof up to a depth of 300 meters and featured
circular white gold hour markers on the dial. The
GMT Master also made its debut in the 1950s, with a
dual time zone feature that used a two-hand system:
the main hand indicated the hour on the twelve-hour
ring, while the other hand indicated the hour on the
twenty-four hours of the rotating bezel. After the Rolex
"dual time zone" came, in 1983, the GMT Master II,
which could display up to three different time zones.

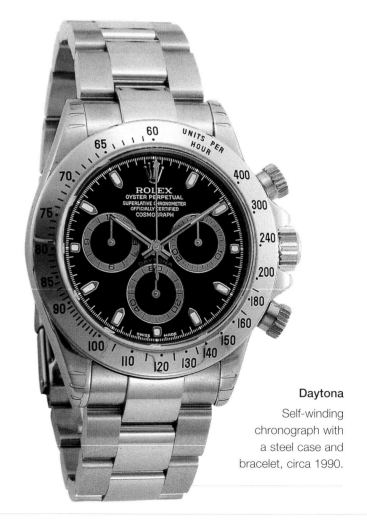

Daytona

Self-winding
chronograph with
a steel case and
bracelet, circa 1990.

1953 also saw the introduction of the Explorer: with a black dial, no calendar and large Arabic numerals alternating with geometric hour markers, this model took part in one of history's legendary feats, worn by New Zealander Edmund Hillary when he conquered the world's highest peak, Mount Everest. From the loftiest peaks to the deepest abysses: on January 23, 1960, the Trieste bathyscaphe, with Jacques Piccard and the American lieutenant Don Walsh on board and a Rolex Deep Sea Special attached to the exterior, set a new record for underwater descent, diving to a depth of 10,916 meters in the Pacific Ocean's Mariana Trench.

In 1961, the Oyster Cosmograph arrived on the scene, a source of joy and torment for Rolex chronograph fans, with a tachymetric scale on the bezel and "pump" style buttons: the Daytona was born. The many modifications made to the model over its history include screw-down chronograph buttons, dials with contrasting timers, bezels in steel or impressed on a black background and the most precious and sophisticated variation of them all, the "Paul Newman", with a dial made unusual by the fact that the border of the minute scale is the same color as the timers. In the technical arena, the first manual-winding mechanisms were followed, in 1988, with a self-winding version developed from the Zenith El Primero and, in 2001, the self-winding Daytona chronograph was equipped with a caliber made entirely in-house.

Oyster "Little Egg"

Self-winding watch with a steel case, circa 1930.

The most important developments in more recent years include the Sea-Dweller, which can be considered the quintessence of technology in the service of underwater activity, thanks to the input provided by the professional divers who collaborated on its design, resulting in the further improvement of the already exceptional qualities of the Submariner. The first version was released in 1971, waterproof up to a depth of 610 meters and complete with a helium valve, followed by the Sea-Dweller, with double the impermeability. Other champions of the 1970s include the Oysterquartz, worn on the wrist of mountaineer Reinhold Messner during his "eight-thousanders", and the Explorer II, a dual time zone with a fixed twenty-four-hour steel bezel.

The most recent innovations, continuing in the direction of design continuity and the almost invisible improvement of the watch range, include the Rolex Yacht-Master of 1992, the reissue of the 1930s Prince models, featuring evocative lines and solutions of strong aesthetic and mechanical impact, as well as the series celebrating the fiftieth anniversary of the Submariner and the GMT, respectively, the "green bezel" Submariner of 2003 and the gold GMT Master II with a ceramic bezel, presented at the Basel Fair in 2005.

Submariner
Self-winding watch with a steel case and bracelet.

Submariner "Green Bezel"
Self-winding watch with a steel case and bracelet, waterproof up to 300 meters.

Yacht-Master
Self-winding watch with a steel case and bracelet and a platinum bezel and dial.

Explorer
Self-winding watch with a steel case and bracelet.

1

Oyster Perpetual Yacht Master II

Self-winding chronograph with programmable countdown, instant synchronization and a gold case and bracelet.

2

Oyster Perpetual Cosmograph Daytona

Self-winding chronograph with column wheel, chronometer certification, gold case and leather strap.

3

Oyster Perpetual Datejust II Rolesor

Self-winding watch with central seconds, date in window on dial and quick correction, steel and gold case and bracelet.

4

Oyster Perpetual Explorer II

Self-winding watch featuring a second time zone indication with quick correction and separate from the hours, steel case and bracelet.

1

2

3

4

Prince

Manual-winding
mechanical
watch with a gold
case, a back
that reveals the
mechanism and
an alligator strap.

A curious variant was introduced in the form of the 2007 Milgauss. Its Oyster case faithfully followed the anti-magnetic principles of the models built starting in the 1950s, but the version with the black dial featured, in a special edition, a green sapphire crystal. Technology became one of the Rolex musts, introducing, with the Yacht-Master II, a new complication for seafarers: the regatta chronograph. It was a development highly appreciated by collectors, and doubled in 2012 with the Sky-Dweller, featuring dual time zone, annual calendar and a rotating bezel that, like the Yacht-Master II, became an essential practical element of the watch. 2012 was the year in which Rolex sealed its supremacy in the area of impermeability.

Fifty years after its first adventure, Rolex returned to the Mariana Trench, this time with the Oyster Perpetual Deepsea Challenge, an experimental model with guaranteed watertightness up to 39,370 feet (12,000 meters). An evolution of the Rolex Deepsea of 2008 (impermeable up to 3,900 meters), this design, fabricated in a single piece with a steel case and titanium back, was 51.4 millimeters in diameter, 28.5 millimeters thick and had a self-winding mechanism. The Rolex Deepsea Challenge was an active participant in the expedition carried out by James Cameron, Explorer-in-Residence of the National Geographic Society and internationally renowned film director (his film "The Titanic" won the Oscar in 1998), who touched the deepest part of the ocean on March 26, 2012 on board the Deepsea Challenger submarine.

**Oyster Perpetual
Sky-Dweller**

Self-winding watch with
dual time zone, annual
calendar, seventy-two
hour power reserve
and a white gold case
and bracelet.

The plastic watch revolution was driven by Swatch. The sheer structural simplicity of the watch design conceals a combination of innovation and high technology, art and color, communication and marketing.

Swatch

1983 was a fundamental year for horology. After the invasion of digital models with Japanese quartz calibers (and the consequential crisis in Swiss manufacturing), the homeland of watches developed its own countermeasures for holding back the tide. The attempt to beat the Japanese colossi at their own game, fabricating low-cost quartz mechanisms, failed: to reconquer its former splendor, it was necessary instead to find a new interpretive key, one that was truly innovative in both content and price point. The leader of this endeavor was, for the strategic and financial side, Nicolas G. Hayek, while the practical aspects were handled by Ernst Tomke, Elmar Mock and Jacques Muller, the three engineers behind the idea of Swatch. Basing their work on research done by ETA (a company specialized in developing watch movements) at the end of the 1970s for the ultra-thin Delirium caliber (just 0.98 millimeters thick), the designers created a mechanism with the same structural philosophy. The elements of the case also had to have a functional purpose: which is why the back became the bottom plate for the caliber. Using innovative techniques, including the microextrusion of the plastic materials, it was possible to reduce the number of components from ninety-one (as in a traditional quartz watch) to

Opposite

Folon Le Temps, Perspective and **Voir**

Swatch Art, designed by Jean Michel Folon, 1987.

The red and white cross flag of the Swiss Federation on the Typical Square dial, 2000.

Referenza GR100

Electronic quartz watch in red plastic, 1983.

Jelly Fish

Electronic quartz watch with a completely transparent case, 1984.

White Horse

Electronic quartz
chronograph in plastic
with a multicolor
dial, 1990.

fifty-one, with the undeniable advantage of simplified fabrication and a smaller production chain, which in turn permitted considerable economies of scale. The plastic case, partnered with colorful buckle straps, distinguished the launch of the Swatch era, and at its launch on March 1, 1983, the Swatch watch stunned the industry with its extremely low price (about twenty-five euro) and high quality construction: the analog quartz movement was guaranteed to fluctuate no more than one second per day, the case was waterproof up to thirty meters and, if the watch malfunctioned within the warranty period, the customer would immediately receive a replacement.

The first single-color options (red, yellow, black and green) were followed in 1984 by multicolor models, which had an appealing, almost subversive aesthetic: this was the consecration of the product, which placed the Swiss Made ("Swatch" derives from the combination "Swiss + Watch") at the top of watch-lovers' favorites. The driving force of Swatch was also felt by other Swiss manufacturers who, after a long creative standstill, recaptured their strength on the wave of the success of the plastic watch, returning to the top of their game and relaunching the entire industry. Swatch is to be considered the most extraordinarily revolutionary product in contemporary watchmaking, having introduced a new way of thinking about watches, which had been up until then preserved with the utmost care and seen as a precious companion for life and a unique and fundamental instrument for describing the passage of time. Swatch instead offered an urban style and the pleasure of constant change: time told on the wrist could now be experienced through continually updated technological solutions and a high-impact look, becoming a manifesto of colorful vitality to accompany wearers in their everyday lives.

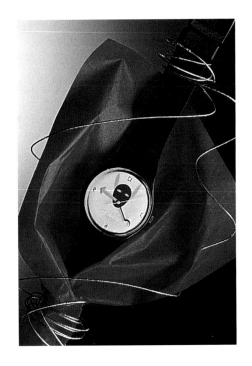

Oigol Oro Mimmo Paladino

One of the Art Swatch watches most coveted by collectors, produced in an edition of 140 numbered pieces.

Haring Serpent, Mille Pattes and Blanc sur Noir Swatch Art, designed by the graffiti master Keith Haring, 1986.

I n addition to young designers, the leaders of a constantly evolving graphic style, Swatch also called upon major artists who, with their passion and inventive spirit, dedicated themselves to this ultramodern timepiece, transforming it into a rich palette for experimentation: designs by Folon, Mimmo Paladino, Arnaldo Pomodoro, Valerio Adami and the biggest names in painting, sculpture and photography lent an intellectual aura to the brand. The classic

Kiki Picasso

Swatch Art, designed by the French artist Christian Chapiron (known by the pseudonym Kiki Picasso), 1985.

The model Valeria Mazza
wearing Swatch for
the opening of the
Swatch boutique
on Via della Spiga,
in Milan, Italy.

Jelly Skin

Skin, 1998.

Pure Line

Skin, with a case
thickness of just 3.9
millimeters, 1997.

Shadiness

Skin Beat,
with a digital
display, 2000.

Phenomenon

Skin Chrono,
electronic quartz
chronograph,
2001.

triple sphere with calendar was quickly joined by other watch types: the self-winding model became the first standard bearer of Swatch's mechanical vocation, while the waterproof Scuba and especially the Chrono brought the company continually increasing success and global sales. Swatch's distinctive characteristic lies in its capacity to surprise, even introducing steel and aluminum cases (for the Irony collection). The Skin line, distinctive for the thinness of its case (3.9 millimeters), was followed, starting in 2003, by the Swatch Touch models, which were operated via a special tactile technology, reaffirming the company's primacy in the area of research and development, a fundamental characteristic of the brand.

In support of Swatch's philosophical importance and its vocation for grasping the true spirit of the times, the brand responded to the intergenerational trend of the 1990s with Internet Time. Swatch Beat was in fact the first wristwatch that did not use the classic division of the day into twenty-four sixty-minute hours, instead introducing a new unit of time, tied to the world of the Web and expressed in Swatch Beats, an initiative supported by communications gurus (including Nicholas Negroponte, the founder of the Massachusetts Institute of Technology's Media Lab and a leading media scholar), for finding a new way of measuring time that would better serve "net" time.

Swatch's Internet Time divided the day into 1,000 units, each corresponding to a beat, equaling 1 minute, 26.4 seconds each. "Noon" is indicated by @500 Swatch Beats and, for getting synchronized based on your geographic position, the reference is the alternative meridian in Biel (the Swiss city where the Swatch headquarters are located), replacing GMT with BMT (Biel Mean Time). The ultramodern and rigorously digital Swatch Beat watches have been produced in

Black Sceptre
Irony collection, electronic quartz, 2002.

Happy Joe Yellow
Irony Big, steel case, 1997.

support of this initiative since the late 1990s, which while intriguing from the intellectual point of view, have had little commercial impact. Sometimes Swatch watches cross over into the most prestigious materials, like the Trésor Magique, which has a platinum case, or the diamond-decorated Nuit Etoilée and Lustrous Bliss, while, from the technical perspective, the most transgressive design is undoubtedly the Diaphane One of 2001, a limited edition watch celebrating Abraham-Louis Breguet's invention of the tourbillon. The principle of the rotating cage, which in a tourbillon functions to compensate for the timing errors caused when the watch changes vertical position, was applied to the Diaphane One, distinguished by a transparent dial revealing a rotating cage. This cage, which was different from the tourbillon cage in that its mechanism had more components, completed a full rotation every thirty minutes, with a second hand, positioned on a special small dial, rotating around the central hour and minute hands. The case, which was notably thick, was made of translucent plastic and aluminum, with a porthole style back in sapphire glass, revealing the caliber A93.001, a manual-winding caliber composed of 164 elements.

From left to right:

Reference GN701
With date and day of the week, 1983.

Don't Be Too Late
With a plastic case, 1984.

Reference GB103
Dial with large numbers, 1983.

Black Magic
With an all-black case and dial, and contrasting hands, 1984.

I n the area of specialized progress, Swatch has distinguished itself for the introduction of intriguing solutions integrating the indication of time with special functions, like the Access Snowpass, the first wrist ski pass, with a microchip inside for storing data and an antenna for opening the gate at ski lift entrances. The brand's tie with the world of sports is confirmed through pairings with some of the most popular sports, especially those loved by young people, and has been powerfully reinforced through the company's role as the Official Timekeeper at some of the more recent Olympic Games.

Download
Beat, 1999.

Webstream Black
Irony Beat, 1999.

Diaphane One

Manual-winding watch with a special mobile cage device and a plastic and aluminum case, 2001.

Bluematic

Self-winding watch in blue plastic, 1991.

The Fun Scuba of 2004 instead features a plastic case designed to be exceptionally watertight (guaranteed up to 200 meters) and equipped with a depth meter that, although it makes no claim to being a substitute for the professional computer used by divers, instantly indicates depth during dives. Swatch has an endless capacity to renew itself and has sold hundreds of thousands of watches, demonstration of the global success of a brand that changed the history of watchmaking through the genius and creative use of plastic.

Blue Trap and **Wind Up**

Diaphane
Automatic, 2004.

Climbing Lobster

Fun Scuba collection, electronic quartz watch with depth meter, in multicolor plastic, 2004.

Yellow Butterfly

Fun Scuba collection, waterproof up to 200 meters, 2004.

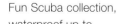

Bora-Bora

Scuba collection, electronic quartz watch, plastic, 1990.

Colours Code

The ten models of a 2010 collection
that brought back the original pieces
designed by the brand that revolutionized
the watch industry in the 1980s.

Swiss Avant-Garde since 1860. The Tag Heuer slogan emphasizes the watchmaker's commitment to quality, producing designs aimed to push the boundaries of precision. Sports performance, with a special propensity for speed, is what inspires the house to improve the mechanical technology of its watches.

TAG Heuer

douard Heuer founded the business in 1860 in Saint-Imier, which nine years later debuted its first patent for a special manual winding system. Heuer has been synonymous with reliable movements right from the start, meeting the demand for precision set by the nascent sports activity of the modern age. In 1887, the house patented the oscillating pinion chronograph, a system still used today by many prestigious manufacturers. Its focus

The American actor Steve McQueen during the filming of Le Mans in 1971, wearing a Heuer Monaco.

on the chronograph led Heuer to win a silver medal at the Universal Exposition in Paris at the end of the nineteenth century. The next century opened at Heuer with the pulse meter dial, which made it easier to read the pulse. And the company's tie to the car racing world began with the introduction of a dashboard time-piece complete with an indication of trip duration. In 1916, Heuer presented the Micrograph, the first mechanism capable of keeping time with a precision up to one one-hundredth of a second: this was, however, a sports timer and not a complete watch. Heuer's competence in measuring short-term phenomena was recognized in 1920, when the company's devic-

Opposite
Steve McQueen Monaco

Self-winding chronograph with a steel case.

Left
Monaco

Manual-winding chronograph with a steel case, 1974.

Right
Monaco

Self-winding mechanical chronograph, steel case.

es were chosen as the timers for the Olympic Games in Antwerp. Heuer's participation as the Official Timekeeper continued in 1924 in Paris and 1928 in Amsterdam, returning again to the role in Lake Placid and in Moscow in 1980.

Microtimer

Electronic quartz movement, accurate to one one-thousandth of a second.

I n 1930, the manufacture presented a new dashboard timepiece with an hour timer, followed by the first multi-timer chronograph. The Autavia dashboard timepiece dates to 1933, a legendary design that would be interpreted in a number of wristwatch models with highly distinctive characteristics. After World War II, the company unveiled the Mareograph, a wrist chronograph that could indicate the tides. Heuer became synonymous with technical quality and instruments for extreme sports, which required maximum levels of precision: 1964 was the year of the Carrera chronograph, a history-maker in contemporary sports horology. With a dual-timer dial, this model was used for the first time in the grueling Carrera Panamericana car race, which wound for 3,000 kilometers from the extreme north of Mexico to Guatemala. In 1969, the Carrera was the first watch to be equipped with the Caliber 11, a mechanism that self-wound using an integrated micro-rotor. This movement, developed in collaboration with Buren and Hamilton, competed with the Zenith El Primero caliber in the race to produce the first self-winding chronograph.

Caliber 360

Self-winding chronograph with a balance wheel that oscillates at 360,000 vibrations/hour, ensuring accuracy to one one-hundredth of a second, the maximum currently possible for a mechanical watch; TAG Heuer prototype.

Heuer then designed the Microtimer (1966), a small-size electronic precision timing instrument that could measure time up to one one-thousandth of a second and, in the 1970s, the house was the official timekeeper for the Ferrari Formula 1 team. In 1975, the company presented the Chronosplit, the first quartz chronograph with both LED and LCD digital display.

1985 was the year of a major turn: Heuer formed an alliance with TAG (Techniques d'Avant-Garde), a leader in experimental research. This was the birth of TAG Heuer, with headquarters in Marin. The first result of this technological partnership was the Formula 1 model. The star of this collaboration with the world of cars and high speed was Alain Prost, a TAG Heuer brand ambassador in 1985, the year in which the French racer won the world championship. In 1987, TAG Heuer made its debut at the Alpine Skiing World Cup, sponsoring champions including Marc Girardelli and Helmut Hoeflehner and unveiled the S/EL (short for Sport/Elegance) sports watch line. The Series 6000 chronograph of 1994 was voted watch of the year and worn by Ayrton Senna, the undisputed and unforgettable racing champion and TAG Heuer brand ambassador. In the second half of the 1990s, the house won over aficionados for its almost exclusive production of sports watches. TAG Heuer's collections fell into two distinct categories: technical and innovative watchmaking, represented by the 2000 series and Kirium, and, on the other hand, the Classics, expressed in collections like Monaco and Carrera. The Monaco was a self-winding chronograph with a square case and a reissue of the model worn by Steve McQueen in the 1970 film "Le Mans", while the Carrera followed the lines of the first model, designed for the Panamericana race.

Monaco V4

Movement with four barrels and belt energy distribution, inspired by car design; TAG Heuer prototype.

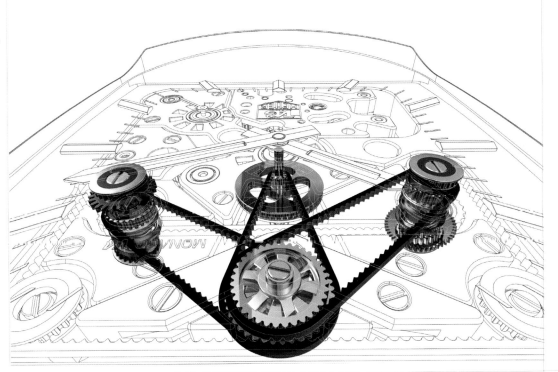

In 1999, TAG Heuer was acquired by the LVMH group, which maintained the strategies of the Marin house and expanded its existing lines, continuing to sponsor sporting events and sports champions, who were selected as brand ambassadors. In 2001, the Classics line was expanded to include the Monza collection, a chronograph with a carré galbé case, while the sports models were worn by Tiger Woods, the international golf champion, and the athletes on the BMW Oracle Racing team in the America's Cup. TAG Heuer then reissued the Autavia, with a case that recalled that of the 1960s original and with the chro-

The Carrera Panamericana Mexico race in a vintage photograph.

Carrera

Manual-winding steel chronograph, "pump" style buttons, baton indices and hands, circa 1960.

The original poster for the Carrera Panamericana Mexico race, a challenging and adventurous reliability trial that, due to its dangerousness, was only held for a few years between 1950 and 1960.

Autavia

Self-winding mechanical chronograph, caliber 11, 1969.

nograph buttons on the side opposite the winding crown. In the area of innovation, in 2002, the company introduced the Microtimer, featuring a quartz movement accurate to one one-thousandth of a second and an extremely elegant and refined look, winner of the Prix du Design at the Grand Prix d'Horlogerie de Genève. In 2004, the Monaco V4 was unveiled, the prototype for a mechanical watch defined by its revolutionary technology. The latest frontier conquered by TAG Heuer is represented by the Caliber 360, the first mechanical wrist chronograph to measure one one-hundredth of a second and presented in prototype form at the 2005 Basel Fair, with a round titanium case and a natural rubber strap.

Carrera Tachymeter

Self-winding chronograph with a steel case and bracelet, calendar and tachymetric scale engraved on the bezel.

Carrera

The complete series of self-winding steel chronographs.

Carrera 1964

Self-winding steel chronograph, limited edition of 1964 pieces in celebration of the model's fortieth anniversary.

The Monaco V4 finally became a reality, destined for the wrists of a few lucky watch lovers in 2009, in a limited series of 150 pieces celebrating the 150th anniversary of the house. The company's experimentation continued, resulting in new surprises like the Grand Carrera Caliber 36 RS Caliper, which can measure time with an accuracy of one-tenth of a second, and the Pendulum, a revolutionary model which uses a "virtual" spring instead of a hairspring, characterized by a low angle of oscillation. The increasingly accurate measurement of time was the theme around which the Carrera Mikrograph 100 and the Mikrotimer Flying 1000 were designed, with the former featuring a large chronograph hand signaling one one-hundredth of a second and the latter one one-thousandth. Current production exploits major technical improvements, with models like the Monaco Chronograph which abandons Plexiglas in favor of the more modern sapphire glass and the Carrera that, in a few special variations, features indications driven by the Caliber 1887, a mechanical design refined and industrialized by TAG Heuer's master watchmakers.

Carrera Caliber 1887

Self-winding chronograph with calendar, a waterproof steel case, anthracite dial, alligator strap the same color as the dial and rose gold color hands and numbers.

Aquaracer Caliber 5 Full Black

Self-winding watch waterproof up to 500 meters, titanium case with a black titanium carbide coating, helium valve, graduated rotating bezel and natural rubber strap.

Heuer Carrera Mikrograph

Self-winding chronograph with chronometer certification, measures 1/100 second increments thanks to a balance that vibrates at 360,000 beats per hour, rose gold case; limited series of 150 pieces.

Monaco V4

Self-winding platinum watch in a
limited series of 150 pieces, with
an innovative system of transmitting
power via belts and a linear

Tissot's skill in identifying itself with imagination and creativity is emphasized by its company slogan, Innovators by Tradition, which since 1853 has stood revolutionary technical developments and the use of unconventional materials, like plastic in the 1970s and granite in the 1980s.

Tissot

Tissot, one of the most traditional Swiss manufactures, was founded in 1853 in Le Locle, a town located in the Jura Mountains. Established by Charles-Félicien Tissot, the company produced pocket watches and, thanks to Charles-Emile Tissot, the founder's son, became one of the watchmakers with the most business activity outside Switzerland.

Print advertisement, circa 1935.

In 1858, Charles-Emile left Le Locle for Russia: the land of the Czars was Tissot's primary market at that time, but the company also exported to various European countries, the United States and countries in Latin America. Tissot watches won numerous awards and prizes at the Expositions in Paris, Antwerp and Geneva, and VIPs of the period, including the actress Sarah Bernhardt, chose the house as their preferred watch brand. Tissot was an important contributor to the wristwatch revolution, presenting interesting models like the Prince (1917), called the Banana for its unusual arched case and Art Deco numerals on the dial, and those with antimagnetic cases, typical of the 1930s, which were the watch world's technical answer to needs imposed by industrial technology. Those were the years of the spread of the telephone and electrical appliances, tools that were extremely useful in everyday life but that were also sources of magnetic fields and therefore the enemies of watch mechanisms, which could not function properly when affected by magnetism.

Navigator

Self-winding chronograph with world time indication and a steel case, 1952.

Opposite

Astrolon – Idea 2001 by Tissot Research

Manual-winding watch with a mechanism and case in a synthetic material, 1971.

Wood Watch

Electronic quartz watch with a heather wood case and dial, 1989.

Print advertisement for the Tissot Rock Watch, circa 1980.

In the 1940s, Tissot launched intriguing publicity campaigns to promote and market its products: in Switzerland, the company partnered with the best shops in the major cities to offer a direct look at the complexity of the mechanism, putting a technician specialized in precision adjustment in the shop window. It was an interesting and entertaining initiative. The brands successive promotional activity was especially focused on sports sponsorship: yachting in 1966, car racing at the end of the 1960s and, more recently, bicycling, motorcycling, fencing and ice hockey, with Tissot as the Official Timekeeper.

Print advertisement for the Tissot Rock Watch, circa 1980.

Demonstration of the authentic innovative spirit of the brand has, however, always been the purview of its products. Starting with the Navigator in 1953, a world time model distinguished for its practical beauty and user-friendliness, with a dial divided into twenty-four sectors corresponding to the world's twenty-four time zones, a monumental version of which, the World Watch, was set up at the Royal Saltworks at Arc-et-Senans, a UNESCO World Heritage site. The Navigator was later presented by

Rock Watch

Electronic quartz watch with a granite case and dial, 1985.

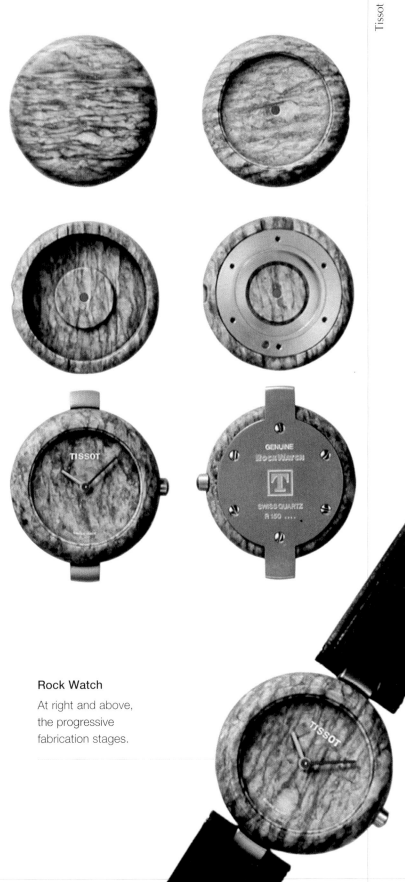

Rock Watch

At right and above, the progressive fabrication stages.

Tissot in an electronic, or, more specifically, digital, version. The PR516 of 1965 was aesthetically inspired by the world of cars, or better, the design of sports car steering wheels. Special note should be made of the brand's 1968 publicity campaign, which saw the Tissot logo plastered on the side of a car driven by the Peruvian champion, Henry Bradley. In 1978, the tie with the world of speed racing would be renewed through a partnership with Lotus, a Formula 1 team managed at the time by the legendary Colin Chapman. The decision to use innovative materials dates to the 1970s, with the Tissot Sytal (which was marketed in Italy also under the names Idea 2001 and Tissot Research), a forerunner for the Swatch watch, featuring a mechanism, called the Astrolon, made in large part out of plastic. The possible advantages of greater production efficiency and appreciable reduction in the lubrication of the movement's movable parts corresponded, however, with scant success: the Sytal was very probably too ahead of its time and the solutions proposed by the designers were not yet able to guarantee the levels of reliability needed in a wristwatch. It was a completely different story for the Rock Watch, which was a great success. This model was sculpted from stone, at first granite from the Swiss Alps (1985), then rock from mountains all over the world, but all of the variations were given the same distinctive red and yellow hands. Other models made out of unusual materials were produced in 1987 and 1988, specifically, the Pearl Watch and the Wood Watch, which featured, respectively, mother-of-pearl and Mediterranean heather wood dials. Ceramic made its debut in 1991 with the Tissot Ceraten, with a electronic quartz movement and a lithium battery guaranteed to last more than ten years. This model was followed by the Titanium 7, made out of titanium and featuring a dual time zone complication. The multiple time zone function was a Tissot specialization, other models including the Two Timer of 1986, which introduced the display of both digital and analog time and for which all of the functions were controlled by a single crown. The new entry in 2000 was the T-Touch: with this watch, by simply touching its screen with your finger, you could activate all of the watch functions beyond the indication of time and date, including altimeter, chronograph, compass, alarm clock, barometer and thermometer.

Print advertisement for the F1, circa 1970.

F1

Electronic quartz watch with digital and analog display and a steel case and bracelet, circa 1978.

T-Touch

Electronic quartz watch
with a touch screen,
a steel case and a
natural rubber strap.

Heritage Black Bay

Watch with self-winding mechanical movement, waterproof up to 200 meters, steel case, natural rubber strap and graduated rotating bezel with immersion times in claret red.

Long considered the Rolex group's second brand, in 2007 Tudor launched a important new design direction. The brand is distinctive for its intriguing collections and a strategy focused on total creative and manufacturing independence.

Tudor

Fastrider

Self-winding chronograph with a mechanical movement, steel case with an alternation of satin and shiny finishes, red dial and fabric strap, forty-six-hour power reserve.

Right

Two other versions of the Fastrider self-winding chronograph: one with a steel case and bracelet and the other with a steel case and fabric strap, both with a tachymetric scale engraved on the bezel.

The brainchild of Hans Wilsdorf, who after founding Rolex wanted to develop a brand with the same structural characteristics and distinguished for high reliability but with a lower price point, for years Tudor played a secondary role in the house of the five-point crown. A position that the brand grew out of in recent years, with entirely new management setting Tudor on an independent path marked by significant development and a well-organized product range distinctive for its strong personality.

The brand's origins date to 1926, the year in which the Tudor name was registered, but it was not until twenty years later that Montres Tudor SA was established in Geneva. In 1947, the first Tudor Oyster models and the Oyster Prince line entered production. The rose logo, symbolic of the royal English dynasty that inspired Wilsdorf, was replaced with a stylized shield, adopted in 1969 for the launch of the Tudor Prince Submariner and the Prince Date-Day models. In the 1970s, the brand introduced its first chronograph lines, while the Monarch and Hydronaut collections were unveiled in, respectively, 1991 and 1999.

2007 was Tudor's watershed year. The eloquent signs of a strong desire for independence were found in powerfully distinctive products supported by an international press campaign. The Grantour line, inspired by the world of sports, the Tudor Glamour Double Date models for those with more traditional taste and the vintage style of the Heritage Chrono, Advisor and Black Bay models were accompanied by important partnerships, especially in the world of car racing, as the timing partner for Porsche Motorsport and Ducati.

A house dedicated to chronography and chronometry, Ulysse Nardin brought the fascination of astronomical complications inherited from the monumental clocks of the past into its own time. Transferring the planets from the facades of historic buildings to wristwatch dials.

Ulysse Nardin

Born on January 22, 1823, Ulysse Nardin inherited his passion for horology from his father, becoming over the years an expert interpreter of the mechanical art of time. The house was founded in 1846, the year in which the first Ulysse Nardin models appeared. The company's production stood out for the high structural quality of its pocket watches and especially its marine chronometers, a well-known specialty of the manufacture. Precision and reliability have always been the company's distinctive qualities, and its history is studded with prizes awarded in the sphere of international competitions and Universal Expositions. Added to these are the more than 4,000 recognitions issued by observatories for Ulysse Nardin chronometers, held to be ideal navigation instruments by many Naval divisions.

Medical Chronograph
Single-button chronograph with a chronograph button coaxial to the crown, yellow gold case, manual-winding movement and dial with a medical scale, circa 1930.

Two-button Chronograph
Manual-winding watch with a white gold case, 1942.

175th Anniversary Single-Button
Single-button manual-winding chronograph with a yellow gold case, the reissue of a 1930s model in a limited series of 175 pieces, 1998.

Opposite
Small Seconds
Manual-winding watch with a steel case and fixed articulated horns, circa 1910.

Astrolabium Galileo Galilei
Astronomical watch with a yellow gold case, 1985.

Tellurium Johannes Kepler
Astronomical watch with a platinum case, 1992.

Planetarium Copernicus
Astronomical watch with a yellow gold case, 1988.

At the end of the century, the factory was moved to Le Locle, on Rue du Jardin, which then became the institutional headquarters for the house, and the family tradition continued with Ulysse's son, Paul David Nardin, who contributed much to the company's commercial and technical growth. In the twentieth century, the company unveiled the first wrist chronometers, flanked by self-winding and manual-winding models of extreme aesthetic rigor.

Between the 1960s and 70s, Ulysse Nardin suffered a period of profound crisis, caused by the spread of Japanese quartz mechanisms. Electronics prevailed over traditional mechanical horology and, like other Swiss manufacturers, the company was forced to close its doors.

The turn came in 1983. Rolf W. Schnyder, a Swiss entrepreneur based in Southeast Asia, became fascinated with the noble past of the Ulysse Nardin house, and decided to buy the brand and all that remained of the company. Schnyder started from the ground up, basing his vision on creativity and the desire to amaze, but above all setting the goal of producing technically and aesthetically innovative watches.

Aqua Perpetual
Perpetual calendar self-winding watch, waterproof up to 300 meters, with a steel case and a natural rubber strap.

Marine Perpetual Limited Edition
Perpetual calendar self-winding watch with a steel case and bracelet.

chnyder found the ideal interpreter of his ambitions in Ludwig Oechslin, a brilliant enthusiast of mechanics, astronomy and archeology, and in 1985, the Astrolabium Galileo Galilei was unveiled, a unique and stunningly complex design. It was followed in 1988 by the Planetarium Copernicus, and then the Tellurium Johannes Kepler, creating a trio of wristwatches packed with precise and detailed astronomical information. Oeshslin also worked on typical horology complications, like dual time zone, presented in the practical and functional GMT+/- of 1994 and followed by the Perpetual Ludwig, a perpetual calendar for which all of the indications could be corrected from the winding crown and for which, unique of its kind, the indications could be updated moving them either forward or backward (traditional perpetual calendars can only be adjusted in a forward direction). The Freak and Sonata models are other models resulting from Oechslin's experimentation, the former featuring a mechanism with a new escapement and the latter a GMT with an alarm and a countdown function.

Freak

Manual-winding eight-day watch, carousel with dual direct escapement, rose gold case, 2001. Above, a view of the mechanism, located on the face of the dial.

Sonata

Watch with dual time zone, big date, countdown and alarm, self-winding with a white gold case. Below, a technical drawing of the watch.

Genghis Khan

Watch with tourbillon and minute repeater with automatons and a Westminster Carillon, self-winding, rose gold case and black onyx dial, limited series of thirty pieces, perlage finish bezel, 2002. Below, a close-up of the mechanism, with the tourbillon in the foreground.

One of the leading watchmakers in the 1940s and 50s for the intriguing style it applied to chronography. Tri-Compax, Aero-Compax and Dato-Compax are names preserving the memory of the models of unsurpassed beauty and refinement unveiled by Universal.

Universal Genève

The Universal Genève brand was founded in 1894 in Le Lode. It was in that city that Ulysse Georges Perret and Numa Émile Descombes (the latter later replaced by Louis Berthoud) opened the small business that would later take the name Universal Watch. At first dedicated to pocket watches, in 1917 Universal presented its first wrist chronograph. Meanwhile, the company moved to Geneva. In the 1930s, the economic crisis led to a shift between the descendants of the founders and a group of investors whose financial capacity contributed to transforming Universal into a company with major growth potential. Technical innovation became one of the distinguishing characteristics of the house, with the Compur chronographs flanked by the Compax line, one of the biggest successes in the mechanical watch industry. The debut year was 1936 and the first Compax chronograph introduced a few unusual aspects, like its two buttons (the first was used for start and stop, with the option of restarting and stopping the hand multiple time, while the second was used exclusively for returning to zero) and a totalizing chronometer, which made it possible to exceed the limits of temporal measurement, until then imposed by the minute counter, marked with thirty or five chronograph minutes.

Opposite
Aéro-Compax

From left; gold chronograph, circa 1940; steel chronograph and gold chronograph, circa 1950; steel chronograph with dual time zone, circa 1960.

Compur

Chronograph with square gold case, circa 1940.

Compur

Chronograph with round gold case, created for Hermès, circa 1940.

Polerouter

Waterproof watch with a steel case, rotating bezel with a graduated interior, circa 1960.

Military

Italian Air Force style
chronograph, with a steel
case and flyback function,
produced for Cairelli-
Roma, circa 1950.

Compax

Steel flight
chronograph
with dual time zone,
circa 1940.

Tri-Compax

Steel chronograph
with calendar
and lunar phases,
circa 1950.

Tri-Compax

Gold chronograph
with calendar and
lunar phases,
circa 1950.

The evolution of the house's production was characterized by a long series of chronographs, including the Uni-Compax, the dial of which had no hour counter, and the Aéro-Compax, featuring a patented system comprising a supplementary crown symmetric to the winding crown that was used to adjust the hands of a small auxiliary dial located at twelve o'clock. Once positioned at a precise hour, the hands stayed put without interfering with the functioning of the watch in any way, since the indication was designed solely as a visual reminder, for example, for helping the wearer remember an appointment (this model was also known as the Memento). The little dial at twelve o'clock was later used for the analog display of the date in the Dato-Compax, but the most famous model was certainly the Tri-Compax, unveiled in 1944 in celebration of Universal's fiftieth anniversary. The Tri-Compax was a history-making watch, flanking its three chronograph counters with a complete calendar (with the month and day displayed in a window and analog display of

the date), lunar phases and the tachymetric scale. Universal's innovative capacity also stood out in its non-chronograph models. In 1954, the Polerouter was introduced, a watch designed by Gérald Genta with an antimagnetic case equipped with the Microrotor self-winding caliber (involving an off-center rotor integrated into the mechanism). Originally created to meet the needs tied to the polar air route between Europe and the United States, the Polerouter was later produced in a range of variations.

Cloisonné

Gold and polychrome enamel watch with a map of ancient Egypt and Joan of Arc on horseback, circa 1950.

With the triumph of electronics, during the 1970s, Universal became the European subsidiary of the Bulova Watch Company and dedicated itself to developing quartz mechanisms. In 1988, the Swiss company was acquired by Stelux, a Chinese investment holding company, which focused on reissuing models from the past and, on the house's one-hundredth anniversary in 1994, unveiled the Golden Janus, a watch with a reversible case and a dual time zone complication.

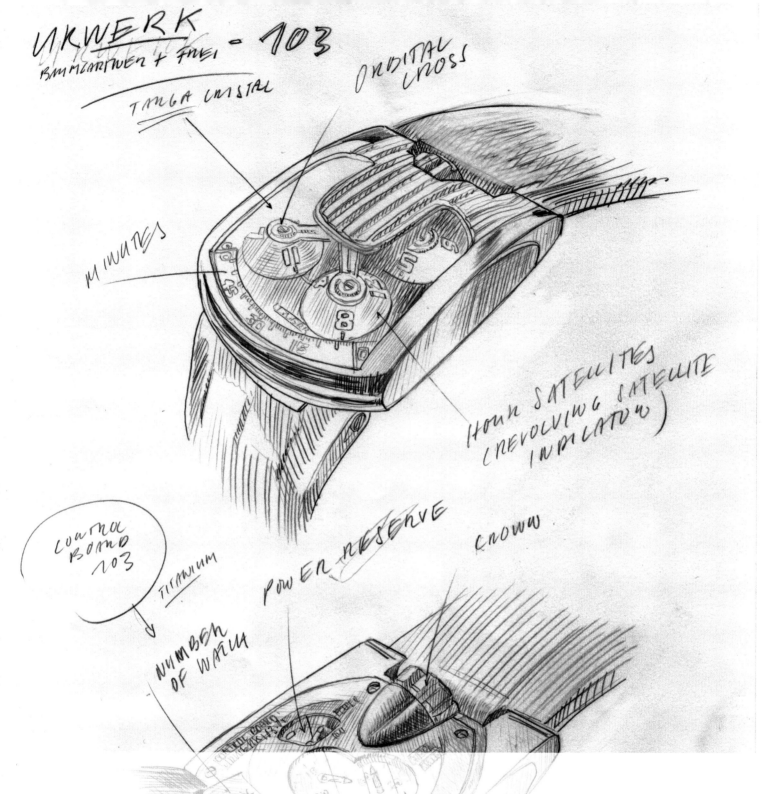

URWERK
BAUMGARTNER + FREI - 103

TANGA CRISTAL

ORBITAL CROSS

MINUTES

HOUR SATELLITES
(REVOLVING SATELLITE
INDICATOR)

CONTROL BOARD 103

TITANIUM

NUMBER OF WATCH

POWER RESERVE

KNOWW

Oneiric visions of the mechanics of time. Urwerk is the realization of a dream: the capacity to forget the shapes and tools of traditional horology, committed to an approach totally outside the box.

Urwerk

Founded in 1995 by designer Martin Frei and the watchmaker brothers Thomas (who later left the company) and Felix Baumgartner, Urwerk is one of the most fascinating contemporary enterprises in the arena of the vision of time. The name pairs that of the ancient city of Ur, where, six thousand years ago, the Sumerians laid the foundations for the division of the solar year into twelve months, with the German word "werk", which means to create, work and shape. Urwerk's style is ultramodern and never banal, and has led the Swiss atelier in the production of innovative, avant-garde watches since 1997. An homage to the great masters is always present in its designs, with the seventeenth-century Campani brothers and their night clocks inspiring the UR-101, a wristwatch with the Arabic numeral relative to the hour moving in a special sector to indicate, with a certain level of approximation but appreciable imagination, the passing of the minutes.

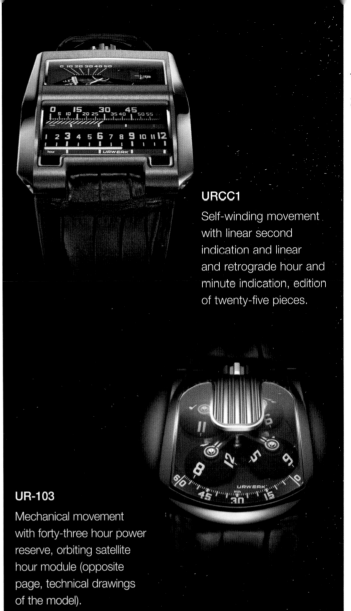

URCC1

Self-winding movement with linear second indication and linear and retrograde hour and minute indication, edition of twenty-five pieces.

UR-103

Mechanical movement with forty-three hour power reserve, orbiting satellite hour module (opposite page, technical drawings of the model).

UR-110

Self-winding movement with satellite indication of hours and an integrated minute hand, day/night indicator.

The continuous evolution of this model was an opportunity for Urwerk to constantly improve its technique, resulting in the UR-102 and, later, the UR-103, distinguished by a satellite display mode, where the hands were transformed into special indicators acting as carousels marking the hours. The dial opens up, specifically in the UR-110 versions and the 200 collection, to reveal transporters, cams and levers that, through a complex movement run by special wheels, transforms cubes, telescopic hands and other components into precise indicators of the hours and minutes.

One of the oldest houses in the horology world, Vacheron Constantin expresses its vocatio[n] for high-end production through models fabricated according to the highest quality, mechanical and stylistic standards. Its signature watch: the ultra-thin manual-wind.

Vacheron Constantin

Geneva, 1755: Jean-Marc Vacheron opens an horology atelier, launching production of pieces with his name imprinted on the dial and mechanism. From the beginning, the company was oriented toward expansion, reaching a wide range of markets, including Russia, Italy and the United States. In 1819, François Constantin joined Vacheron. At first, the new company name was Vacheron & Constantin, with the ampersand being definitively dropped in 1974. In 1839, Georges Auguste Leschot, the inventor of the pantograph (an instrument that totally revolutionized the method of producing horology components), joined the company. Leschot left an indelible mark on nineteenth-century mechanical research, even making appreciable improvements to the winding system and escapement: after all, the house slogan is "Faire mieux si possible, ce qui est toujours possible" (do better if possible, and that is always possible).

In 1880, Vacheron Constantin registered the Maltese Cross as its logo and, in 1911, the company presented its first women's wristwatches, followed two years later by wristwatch models for men. During World War I, the house supplied chronographs and compasses to the American and British militaries. In that period, the company began production of a wide range of wristwatches, in answer to increasing consumer demand for this new type of timepiece. The change in custom led pocket watches to a rapid and unstoppable decline in the 1930s. The first chronograph dates to 1917, with a thirty minute timer and a chronograph button coaxial

1920s

Manual-winding watch with a shaped gold case and Arabic numerals on the dial, circa 1920.

Opposite
Chronograph

Two-button watch with a rose gold case, manual-wind, drop-shaped horns, circa 1930.

"Cioccolatone"

Self-winding watch, carré case with curved sides, circa 1950.

pocket watches and even a few models for the wrist. Technics were no less a focus, with two-button chronographs, complete calendars and perpetual calendars of incomparable elegance, as well as refined minute repeater mechanisms. In addition to the precious metals typical of haute horology, Vacheron Constantin sometimes also used steel and, for a small number of designs, even aluminum. During the company directorship of Georges Ketterer, the charismatic head of the manufacture for more than thirty years starting in 1938, the world's thinnest manual-winding mechanical movement, just 1.64 millimeters thick, was unveiled in celebration of the two-hundredth anniversary of the house: a new level of superiority had been attained in the horology world.

Non-circular time

Manual-winding watch with a rectangular gold case and geometric elements on the sides and horns, convex crystal, circa 1950.

"Cioccolatone"

Self-winding watch with complete calendar and lunar phases and a gold carré case with curved sides, circa 1950.

to the winding crown. A focus on aesthetics became one of Vacheron Constantin's absolute prerogatives, producing models with rectangular, square and imaginatively shaped cases and dials where creativity expressed itself in a rigorous, geometric style or featuring elaborate Roman and Arabic numerals or, for the especially precious pieces, polychrome enamel. The most extreme period of creativity, marked by models distinguished for geometric, Art Deco or Orientalizing elements, coincided with the brand's collaboration with Verger, a jeweler who in the 1920s and 30s contributed to transforming Vacheron Constantin mechanisms into true works of art, creating table clocks,

Between the 1960s and 70s, the company flanked its traditional production with a few models made with quartz movements. In 1972, Vacheron Constantin received the Prestige de la France award for a model with an asymmetrical case, the Structura (reissued in the 1990s in numerous variants, in the 1972 collection), and seven years later the Kallista stunned the industry for the sheer value of the diamonds embellishing the case, dial and bracelet (130 carats overall), totaling about five million dollars at the time. In 1984, Vacheron Constantin was acquired by the Saudi Arabian sheik Ahmed Zaki Yamani, and then in 1996 by Vendôme (which later became the Richemont Group). The house's renewed creative impulse was expressed in a wide range of watch models, like the Les Essentielles line, which included a few ultra-thin (1.2 millimeters) manual-wind designs, the Les Historiques collection, characterized by a return to the masterpieces of the past, and the Les Complications models, featuring complications like perpetual calendar, minute repeater and tourbillon.

Left

Complete Calendar

Watch with rectangular curvex case, complete calendar and lunar phases, circa 1930.

Right

Chronograph

Two-button model with a rose gold case, manual-wind, pulse meter and tachymetric scale, circa 1940.

Minute Repeater

Watch with gold case
and dial with diamond
hour markers,
manual-wind,
minute repeater,
circa 1950.

Enamel Dial

Manual-winding watch
with a gold case and
polychrome enamel dial,
circa 1950.

Ultra-Thin

Manual-winding ultra-thin
watch with a yellow gold
case and baton indices on
the dial, circa 1950.

1996 was the year of the Vacheron Constantin Overseas, a sports watch with a steel case and bracelet and the unusual feature of maintaining its watertightness even when the crown was not screwed into place. Women's models like the Kalla and Egérie jewelry watches were complemented by men's designs that reinterpreted the shapes of the past, updating their diameters and mechanics, through the application of more modern production technologies.

In 2005, Vacheron Constantin celebrated its 250th anniversary, presenting four limited edition wristwatch masterpieces: the Tour de l'Ile, the Saint-Gervais, the Métiers d'Art three boxed collections of four pieces each, with enameled dials) and the Jubilé 1755. The Tour de l'Ile was the summation of the

Ultra-Thin

Manual-winding ultra-thin watch
with a yellow gold case and Roman
numerals on the dial, circa 1950.
Above, the ultra-thin caliber.
Below, a view of the watch
that shows off its thinness.

house's horology heritage. Ten thousand hours of
work were needed to produce this model, an incomparable piece for the technical difficulty of its fabrication, with a manual-winding caliber made up of
834 components. Presented in seven exemplars with
a rose gold case, the two faces of the Tour de l'Ile
(the dial and the back) displayed a complete range
of astronomical information (in addition to perpetual
calendar and equation of time, it had a celestial map
reproducing the position of the stars as observed from
the Earth), without leaving out the great complications of classical horology. The Saint-Gervais instead
introduced the tourbillon with perpetual calendar,
and the unusual feature of an extremely prolonged
power reserve, equal to 250 hours. While the Jubilé
1755, composed of 1,755 pieces, updated one of the
house's strong points: power reserve.

Saint-Gervais

Watch with tourbillon, perpetual calendar and 250-hour power reserve, 55 pieces in platinum, 2005.

Tour de l'Ile

Multi-complication watch with a rose gold case. Indications displayed on the double face. Limited series of seven pieces, 2005. Below, the back of the case.

These wristwatches were complemented by the Esprit des Cabinotiers, only one of which was made, celebrating the genius of eighteenth-century Geneva masters. It was a table clock comprising a lapis lazuli, onyx and gold base topped by a hand-engraved rose gold sphere. Through a secret opening mechanism, the globe opened up, divided into eight "petals", to reveal a clock with a host of complications: perpetual calendar, dual time zone, equation of time, the signs of the zodiac, thermometer and optional automatic chime.

Jubilé 1755

Watch with power reserve, analog display of the day of the week and the calendar. Limited series of 1,755 pieces (252 with platinum cases, 501 with yellow, white or rose gold cases). Below, the self-winding Vacheron Constantin caliber 2475, the mechanical soul of the Jubilé 1755, 2005.

Quai de l'Ile

Annual calendar with retrograde date and lunar phases, case in white gold, self-winding movement.

Patrimony Traditionnelle World Time

Self-winding mechanical watch with all of the world's time zones indicated with their key city names, rose gold case.

Malte

Manual-winding mechanism with tourbillon, Poinçon de Genève and a rose gold tonneau case.

Patrimony Contemporaine

Day and date with retrograde hands, self-winding movement with Poinçon de Genève, rose gold case.

Historique America 1921

Coussin-shaped rose gold case, sand-finished dial and painted numbers, manual-winding mechanical movement.

Métiers d'Art

Dial with enamel decoration inspired by the Dutch artist M. C. Escher (1898–1972), white gold case and self-winding movement, limited series of twenty pieces.

Patrimony Traditionnelle Caliber 2755

Minute repeater with perpetual calendar and power reserve indicator, mechanical movement with tourbillon, platinum case with sapphire glass back.

The next 250 years of Vacheron Constantin manufacture got their start with the introduction of a few new lines distinguished for their high level of creative breadth. The Métiers d'Art collection, dedicated to the celebration of artisan talent through the interpretation of masterpieces of world art, debuted in 2007 with Les Masques. These refined wristwatches had gold dials engraved with faithful reproductions of historic masks in the permanent collection of the Barbier-Mueller museum in Geneva. The next Métiers d'Art creations included the Symbolique des Laques collection, with fine Japanese lacquer decoration by artists from the Zôhiko company in Kyoto, the Chagall & l'Opéra de Paris collection, with Gran Feu enamel dials, and the Les Univers Infinis collection, where the visionary drawings of M. C. Escher were reproduced using a combination of engraving, enamel and inlaid precious stones. Vacheron Constantin is also pure technology, with the Quai de l'Ile of 2008, distinguished for being the first Concept Watch of haute horology. The case, in a contemporary interpretation of the traditional coussin shape, can be customized, using a special software program developed by the Swiss house, to combine the seven elements of the case according to the customer's preferences.

For lovers of technics, the house produced the Patrimony Traditionnelle World Time model, with a crown used for adjusting all of the indications and display of all thirty-seven time zones, and so including not only the traditional twenty-four, but also the half-hour and fifteen-minute time zones.

Continuous evolution: this is the path that Zenith has followed since 1865, wedding tradition to innovation. A result achieved through the constant technological updating of production cycles and mechanical development.

Zenith

Chronograph

Single-button chronograph, gold case, crown at twelve o'clock, circa 1920.

Military

Mechanical chronograph with a steel case, "pump" style buttons, produced for the Italian Air Force, circa 1960.

Zenith has its origin in the nineteenth century, when Georges Favre-Jacot established his first workshop in Le Locle (1865), introducing methods and systems until then little used in horology, including the interchangeability of pieces between different calibers. Success was immediate, and the business grew and expanded. The company took the name Zenith in 1911 and, as is often the case with manufactures, this name was inextricably linked to that of a caliber designed in that period. The strong development of the house was underlined by the creation, in the Le Locle atelier, of a vast range of pocket watches, wrist models, marine chronometers and mantle clocks, following the principle of increasingly distinguished diversification. Zenith watches were recognized for their precision and reliability, winning prizes and awards at the Universal Expositions in Paris, Milan and Barcelona, as well as other international events.

The house was especially focused on two particular product types, chronometers and chronographs, often confused for their lexical similarity, but substantially different in their functional characteristics. Chronometers are timepieces marked by consistent performance and distinguished for extremely minimal deviations, such as to pass rigorous precision tests. Chronographs, on the other hand, measure short periods of time, partial or total, which

Diamonds

El Primero self-winding chronograph with a diamond-decorated bezel, circa 1970.

Angular

Self-winding El Primero chronograph with an angular steel case, circa 1970.

Opposite
Chronomaster

Self-winding El Primero chronograph with calendar and lunar phases, circa 1990.

are displayed by hands and counters harmoniously arranged on the dial. Chronographs have played a leading role in the house's production strategy and special mention should be made of those produced during World War II and in successive periods for the French Naval Air Force, the British Navy and the Italian Air Force.

El Primero Espada

Self-winding steel watch with a movement that beats at 36,000 vibrations per hour, waterproof up to 100 meters.

Zenith's greatest period of research coincided with its presentation of the El Primero caliber of 1969, the first integrated self-winding chronograph, with a frequency of 36,000 vibrations per hour (the highest frequency used for a mechanical wristwatch) and distinguished by its high-impact

Chronomaster Open

Self-winding chronograph with
an El Primero movement, power
reserve indicator, steel case
with a window revealing
the mechanics inside.

structural profile, with its chronograph perfectly integrated with the self-winding device. The 1970s crisis shifted Zenith's focus to quartz technology, but the return of fine mechanical horology was merely delayed: in 1989, the El Primero re-entered production, later joined by a reliable, precise ultra-thin self-winding movement, the Elite caliber (1994). The company's collections became increasingly complex, alternating classic models with markedly sporty designs.

The turn came in 1999. That was the year in which Zenith was acquired by the LVMH group, a global luxury holding company, and together they launched a reorganization of the brand oriented toward the highest end of the market. Thierry Nataf and, starting in 2009, Jean-Frédéric Dufour, initiated radical changes in the company's communication and overall strategy, with an increasingly strong focus on internationalization. The Zenith catalog was expanded with major new developments, in collections equally divided between sports models and more traditional watches, standing out among which are pieces with an exceptional technical profile combining the El Primero caliber, perpetual calendar and tourbillon.

Capitain Winsor

Self-winding chronograph with day and month indication and fifty-hour power reserve.

El Primero 1969

Self-winding chronograph with a movement that beats at 36,000 vibrations per hour.

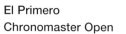

Pilot Doublematic

Self-winding chronograph with world time indication, alarm and big date.

El Primero Chronomaster Open

Self-winding chronograph with column wheel and power reserve indicator.

Pilot Montre d'Aéronef Type 20

Watch with a large titanium case
(57.5 millimeters in diameter) and a
manual-wind movement, indication
of forty-eight hour power reserve
and official chronometer certificate,
limited series of 250 pieces.

Glossary

ADJUSTED: a term inscribed on watch mechanisms and an indicator of the adjustment of the movement itself in one or more positions.

ALARM: an auxiliary mechanism independent of the watch. The device is pointed to the desired time by means of a watch hand. When the watch indicates the selected time, the alarm is triggered and a hammer begins to strike the case or a special drum.

ANALOG: a watch that indicates the time via hands. The other indication type is digital.

ANCHOR: a steel or brass anchor-shaped lever in an escapement.

ANGLAGE:

the creation of an angled edge on a bridge or the rounding of the borders of an opening. This technique is used on high-quality movements.

ANNUAL CALENDAR: a watch that takes into account months with thirty and thirty-one days, thus only requiring date correction for the month of February.

ANTIMAGNETIC:

a watch made out of materials insensitive to magnetism or, more often, made with a movement protected by a magnetic shield, constituted by the dial and a capsule, which covers and surrounds the movement, and made out of extremely pure iron (also called "soft iron").

APERTURE DIAL: a dial with one or more windows (apertures) through which various indications are displayed, like the date, month and day of the week.

BACK:

the back part of a wristwatch case, attached via pressure, screws, a hinge or screwed to the case middle.

BALANCE:

the watch's regulator, comprising a rim (which can be smooth or with screws) and a variable number of arms (between one and four). The oscillations of the balance regulate the rotation speed of the wheel train. The precision of the watch itself depends on the balance's proper functioning.

BALANCE SPRING (HAIRSPRING): an extremely thin, metal Archimedean spiral used to control the oscillations of the balance.

BARREL:

a cylindrical component that houses the mainspring. In wristwatches, the toothed rim of the barrel drives the gear train.

BEZEL: a ring that frames the watch crystal fixed on the top of the watch middle.

BRACELET: a metal "strap" for attaching the watch to the wrist.

BRASS: an alloy combining copper and zinc. It is used in horology to make wheels, plates and bridges.

BREGUET HAIRSPRING (OR OVERCOIL): a spring designed by Breguet, the last spiral of which is lifted up over the others.

BREGUET: the name of the great horologist is used as an adjective for defining watch parts with characteristics introduced by him, such as Breguet hands, Breguet numerals and the Breguet hairspring.

BRIDGE: a metal piece holding bearings within which the upper pivot of the watch's rotating parts turns. To distinguish the bridges, each one is assigned the name of the part that turns below it: the barrel bridge, the anchor bridge and the balance wheel bridge.

BUTTON (PUSH-BUTTON, PUSHER): an element in varied shapes inserted in the watch middle. It is used for the start and stop chronograph functions.

CABOCHON: a rounded precious or semiprecious stone used to decorate the winding crown.

CALENDAR: a watch that reports not only the time, but also date information, presented digitally in small windows or via watch hands (using the analog system).

CALIBER: a term used in horology to designate a range of information: the shape of the movements, the bridges, their number, the origin of the movement, the name of the manufacture, etc.

CARRÉ: a term used to indicate a square-shaped case.

CARROUSEL: a device invented in 1892 by the Danish watchmaker Bonniksen to eliminate performance irregularity caused by the watch's changing positions. Similar to the tourbillon, it has a simpler structure.

CARRURE: a French term describing the middle part of the watchcase.

CASE: an element that contains and protects the watch movement from dust, moisture and blows, also used to give the watch the most attractive appearance possible. The case can comprise two or three separate parts (bezel, case middle, back), and can be made of different materials and in different shapes. Most sports watches have a steel case, while elegant models are in gold or platinum.

CENTRAL EUROPEAN TIME: the standard time, one hour ahead of Greenwich Mean Time, used by many European countries.

CHAPTER RING: a ring, generally attached to the case middle, that displays watch indications (for example markings on diving watches for measuring immersion time).

CHRONOGRAPH:

a mechanism designed to measure the duration of a phenomenon by means of a special hand activated by pressing a button when the phenomenon begins and that can be stopped when the phenomenon ends. Once the measurement is complete, the hand needs to be sent back to zero. The first chronograph proper was invented in 1822 by Rieussec. It was a watch that wrote, via the second hand, the time on a dial, which explains the name given to the new invention: "Chronos" = time, "Grapho" = I write. Instruments of this type were produced for a long period of time, allowing the definition of "chronograph" to remain in use, even though, for the later models, which no longer used a writing device, the name "chronoscope" would have been more accurate. The next phase in the development of the chronograph was led by the Swiss watchmaker Adolphe Nicole, who first completed the chronograph by providing it with a system for returning to zero (1844) and then applied the first mechanism with this function to a pocket watch (1862). The wrist chronograph made its debut in 1910, and was sold by Moeris. Chronographs today can be classified in terms of the connection system used for the chronograph commands. Based on this aspect, one can distinguish the following types: column wheel chronographs, lever chronographs, cam chronographs and oscillating pinion chronographs.

CHRONOGRAPH WITH CALENDAR: a watch with a chronograph function as well as a complete or perpetual calendar.

CHRONOMETER: a watch with elevated precision guaranteed by a chronometer certificate or an official recognition issued by special Swiss observatories.

CHRONOMETER CERTIFICATE: a certificate issued to a manufacture, concerning all of the watches produced by the house that have the same characteristics as sample watches that have been submitted to and passed a series of rigorous tests.

COLUMN WHEEL: a two-part wheel: the lower part is dentelated, while the upper part has trapezoid-shaped vertical columns. In column wheel chronographs, this wheel acts as a "command center" for the various chronograph functions.

COMPLETE CALENDAR: a watch that indicates the date, the day of the week and the month. The date must be updated for all months numbering under thirty-one days. Complete calendar watches often also indicate the lunar phases.

COMPLICATION: a watch function beyond the indication of hours, minutes and seconds.

CORRECTOR BUTTONS: small buttons located on the watch middle used for adjusting the date, day of the week, month, lunar phases, etc. Special pointed tools are used to make these adjustments, designed so that they will not damage the delicate profile of the button.

COSC: an abbreviation of "Contrale Officiel Suisse des Chronomètres" ("Swiss chronometer testing bureau"), a federal authority with headquarters in La Chaux-de-Fonds that tests watches and issues official chronometer certificates.

CROWN: cylindrical element used for winding the watch and adjusting the date and time. For this function, one must first pull the crown slightly away from the case in order to make the adjustments.

DATE (CALENDAR): a supplementary function indicating the day of the month. This information can be indicated through a digital system in a window or using an analog system.

DEAD SECONDS: a device that makes the second hand jump forward every second. This mechanism makes the watch seem like it is run by a quartz movement, when in reality it has a completely mechanical caliber.

DECORATION: the aesthetic elements used to embellish one or more parts of a watch. As for movements, various mechanical methods are used to produce a range of decoration types: perlage, grenage, colima-çonnage, côtes de Géneve and fausses côtes. Dials are decorated using techniques for drawing lines or circles of varying thickness.

DIAL: the part of the watch displaying the hours, minutes, seconds and other indications like astronomical information, the date and power reserve.

DIGITAL: a watch that indicates the time via numbers instead of the traditional hands.

ÉBAUCHE: an unfinished watch movement, missing the balance, escapement, mainspring, dial and hands, but with the gears. The movement is completed by the company that buys it.

ENAMEL DIAL: a copper, silver or gold plate covered in enamel, which is often decorated.

ENAMELING: in horology, this prized polychrome decorative technique, which originated in ancient China, is used to embellish cases, dials and watch backs. The most common techniques are cloisonné and champlevé.

EQUATION OF TIME: calculation of the difference, positive or negative, between solar time and mean time. The two coincide only four times a year, and the Sun can be up to plus fourteen minutes on February 11 and up to minus sixteen minutes on November 4. The difference derives from the eccentricity of the Earth's orbit and the inclination of its axis with respect to the plane of the orbit itself.

ESCAPEMENT: the distributor organ of a watch, fitted between the wheel train and the regulator. It has the task of keeping the balance in motion through impulse and, at the same time, counting the number of oscillations. This is then transformed by the wheel train into time indications. Since the appearance of the first mechanical watch, around two hundred different escapement types have been designed, many of which never left the planning stage and were never produced. Almost all wristwatches use the Swiss lever (anchor) escapement.

FINENESS: the ratio between the weight of a precious metal (gold, platinum) and its total weight in an alloy. Fineness is often expressed in parts per thousand or karats. 24-karat gold or three nines fine gold is pure gold.

FLYBACK: a chronograph mechanism where, if you press the return-to-zero button while the big chronograph hand is in operation, it will be sent immediately back to zero, without having to be stopped first. When you release the return-to-zero button, the chronograph hand starts again.

FREE SPRUNG BALANCE: a balance with a series of screws around its perimeter, making it possible to vary the moment of inertia, and so regulate the rate.

FREQUENCY: the number of oscillations completed by a regulating organ per unit of time (1 second). In a watch, frequency can be expressed in vibrations per hour or in Hertz (one cycle per second). In a movement that completes 18,000 vibrations per hour, the frequency is equal to 2.5 Hz. In horology, the oscillation frequency of regulator organs is expressed in alternations per hour for watches using the balance wheel/balance spring system and in Hertz for quartz watches. One oscillation equals two alternations. One alternation corresponds to the passage of one tooth of the escapement wheel. The most common frequencies in horology are 18,000 A/h or vph—vibrations per hour—(2.5 Hz), 21,600, 28,800 and 36,000. 28,800 and 36,000 A/h (or vph) watches are considered high frequency watches. For quartz watches, the oscillator frequency is 32,768 Hz.

G.M.T. (GREENWICH MEAN TIME): an abbreviation indicating the mean time for the Prime Meridian, corresponding with the location of the Greenwich Observatory.

GALBÉ: a French term used to describe the concave or convex curve of a dial or case.

GLUCYDUR: an alloy made of copper and beryllium with good mechanical characteristics (elastic, durable, non-magnetic). Glucydur is often used to make balance wheels.

GOLD: in horology, this precious metal, known for its flexibility and incorruptibility, is used to make cases, bracelets, bezels, crowns and a few elements of the movement.

GUILLOCHÉ: an engraved geometric design used to decorate dials, made up of intersecting lines that create small lozenges.

GYROMAX: a sophisticated balance wheel with little, turnable weights, a small part of which has been cut out, recessed into the rim. Rotating the cutout side toward the interior decreases speed, while the opposite increases speed.

HANDS:

elongated elements in various styles, usually made of metal, that display the watch's analog indications.

HERTZ (HZ): a unit of frequency. The frequency of a periodic phenomenon equal to one cycle per second.

HORNS: the part of the case connecting the case middle of a wristwatch to the element for attaching the strap.

HOUR COUNTER: a subsidiary dial indicating elapsed hours.

HUNTER: a watch with a metal cover that protects the watch crystal.

INDEX (REGULATOR): a device the position of which can be regulated such as to modify the watch's rate by varying the effective length of the balance spring, increasing or decreasing speed. An especially refined index regulator is the "swan's neck regulator", which allows finer adjustments by means of a screw.

INDEXES: stylized elements, precious stones or Arabic or Roman numerals used to indicate the hours and minutes on the dial.

JEWELS (RUBIES): bearings made of precious stone (rubies, diamonds, sapphires) or artificial stone (syn-

thetic rubies) used in watch movements to reduce friction and wear and better preserve the watch's lubricating oil.

JUMP:

a watch with special windows on the dial showing the hours and minutes.

LCD (LIQUID CRYSTAL DISPLAY): refers to the liquid crystal dials typical of Japanese quartz watches.

LED (LIGHT EMITTING DIODE): indicates the dials with large numbers characteristic of the first digital quartz watches.

LIGNE PARISIENNE: an old unit of measurement, today used in horology for indicating the dimensions of movements: one ligne equals 2.255 millimeters.

LUG: a small metal rod set between the case horns, used for attaching the watchstrap or bracelet. It can be fixed (soldered to the horns) or mobile.

LUMINESCENT DIAL:

a dial where the numerals or hour markers (and also the hands) are coated with a luminescent substance, making them visible in the dark. Until the 1960s, radium was used, but, once it was discovered to be dangerous, due to the radiation it emits, it was replaced with innocuous substances.

LUNAR PHASES (MOON PHASES): a complication found on the dial of watches that display the date, indicating the various cycles of the moon (called "lunations"), normally presented with a strong focus on aesthetics. Actual lunations last 29 days, 12 hours, 44 minutes and 2.8 seconds, but in wristwatches they are reduced to 29 days and 12 hours.

MAINTENANCE: a system for maintaining the qualities of a watch over time, involving repairs and periodic planned servicing.

MALTESE CROSS: a device that was applied to the barrel cover of some wristwatches in the past, used to regulate the spring inside the barrel and prevent overwinding.

MICROROTOR: a rotor that, instead of being on top of the movement (like in most self-winding watches), is incorporated into the movement in order to reduce its thickness.

MINUTE COUNTER: a small dial on a chronograph with a hand that rotates to indicate the number of rotations (and so the number of minutes) made by the big hand. There are three types of minute counters: 1- continuous: the small hand moves continuously and uniformly; 2- instantaneous: the minute counter hand suddenly jumps to the sixtieth second; 3- semi-in-stantaneous: the hand begins to move around the fifty-eighth second, to then jumps to the sixtieth second. The semi-instantaneous counter is the most common.

MOTION WORK: a wheel train that transforms the movement of the watch's minute wheel, which completes one rotation per hour, to the hour wheel, which completes one rotation in twelve hours.

MOVEMENT: the whole of elements that make up the functional part of a watch, whether mechanical or quartz.

NUMERALS: the numbers on the watch dial.

OSCILLATION: the movement of a balance wheel from one extreme to the other and its return to the starting position. One oscillation equals two alternations or vibrations.

PERPETUAL CALENDAR: a watch that, in addition to the indications of the complete calendar, automatically calculates months with thirty days and February, including Leap Year. Of high mechanical complexity, these watches usually also indicate the lunar phases.

PLATE: a metal plate used as a base for bridges; it has holes for the lower pivots of the watch's various rotating parts.

PLATINUM: the most precious metal in horology. Extremely resistant to blows and external agents, it is used to make cases and bracelets.

POINÇON (HALLMARK):

a hallmark found on the movements of watches that meet precise officially established criteria. The most famous is the Poinçon de Genève, reserved solely for high-quality watches manufactured in Geneva.

POWER RESERVE:

a hand that indicates, in a special area of the dial, the length of time remaining before the watch needs to be rewound.

QUARTZ:

the regulator organ of electronic watches. Quartz is made of silicon dioxide. It vibrates at an extremely high frequency (32,768 Hz in wristwatches, as compared to 2.5–5 Hz for mechanical watches) and its oscillations are very stable. Quartz uses piezoelectricity, through which, submitted to electric tension, it starts oscillating with real mechanical oscillations. Subject to aging, over time, quartz begins to gain time. It is also sensitive to temperature variations: when the temperature increases or decreases, the watch loses time. The number of oscillations is determined by the size and shape of the quartz.

RATTRAPANTE CHRONOGRAPH:

a chronograph with a second chronograph hand, called a rattrapante hand. Watches with this complication have three buttons, two of which are on the case, while the third, which runs the rattrapante hand function, is coaxial to the crown and positioned on another part of the case.

REGULATOR DIAL: a dial with an hours subdial and a seconds subdial placed one above the other within the main dial, which displays the minutes.

REPEATER: a watch complication that chimes the time—hours, quarter hours and minutes—on command (using a special slide or button on the watch middle).

RHODIUM-PLATING: a chemical process used to protect metal objects by coating them with a thin layer of rhodium.

ROTOR:

a semi-circular weight that oscillates thanks to the movement of the watch wearer's arm, thus winding the mainspring of self-winding watches.

ROUND CALIBER: the most common caliber shape. Round calibers are designated by the diameter of the case expressed in ligne (lines) or millimeters.

SCALE: gradations of various kinds, usually positioned around the external band of a chronograph dial. The most common are tachymeter scales, which calculate the speed of moving objects, pulsometer scales, which measure heartbeats, telemeter scales, which calculate the distance of a visible and audible events (such as thunder and gunfire) and slide rules for aeronautic operations.

SETTING MECHANISM: a device used to correct the position of the watch hands.

SHAPED (NON-CIRCULAR) CALIBER: indicates all shapes with the exception of round: oval, square, rectangular, etc.

SHAPED: description of the shape of a non-circular case.

SHOCKPROOF: shockproofing is a special system for protecting the pivot stones on the balance staff, which are protected from blows by jewel bearings. One of the most widely used shockproofing systems is Incabloc®.

SILICON: a non-magnetic, highly resistant material, used in horology for making new-generation balance springs and balance wheels.

SKELETON:

all watch for which all of the various parts of the movement (plate, bridges, etc.) are cut away, and the dial and back are transparent. This gives a certain transparency to the watch. Skeletonizing is almost always, still today, done by hand.

SPORTS TIMERS: chronographs used to measure temporal phenomena, with hands set into motion by buttons controlling the start, stop and return to zero functions. These timers do not tell time, and are produced for various purposes. Based on intended use, some have graduated scales or supplementary indications.

STEEL: an alloy of iron and carbon used especially for wristwatch cases. In recent decades, the industry has preferred stainless steel, a highly resistant alloy of iron, chrome and nickel.

STRAP: an element made of leather, fabric, plastic, natural rubber or other materials, with the task of attaching the watch to the wrist.

SWISS MADE: on the basis of section 2 of Ordinance 232.119 of the Swiss Federal Council on December 23, 1971 concerning the use of the denomination "Swiss" for watches, a movement is considered Swiss if it was assembled in Switzerland, if it was inspected by the manufacturer in Switzerland and if at least fifty percent of the movement's components (the percentage determined by the components' value) were made in Switzerland.

THREE-QUARTER PLATE CALIBER: a caliber in which the gear train, except for the escapement wheel, is under a bridge that covers three-quarters of the plate.

TIME ZONES: the twenty-four sectors, delimited by meridians, into which the globe has been divided so that all of the world's countries can have a standardized time, facilitating international relations.

TIMER:

a special and clearly defined area of the dial, usually circular in shape, that displays indications beyond hours and minutes.

TITANIUM: in horology, this metal's special characteristics of resistance and lightness are exploited in the creation of cases and bracelets.

TONNEAU: a special "barrel" shape and the most typical among non-circular watches.

TORTUE:

a development of the tonneau shape, from which it differs in the flaring of the horns which curve in a way that contrasts with the edges of the dial and lend a sensuous line to the sides of the case.

TOURBILLON:

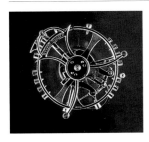

a device invented by Abraham Louis Breguet at the end of the eighteenth century and patented by him in 1801. Its function is to compensate for timing errors caused by the effects of gravity on the balance. It is composed of a rotating cage that holds the escapement, anchor and balance. This cage completes a full rotation around its own axis at a variable rate, having the same rotation center as the balance. You can thus observe how the balance continuously changes position, as if the entire watch were turning around itself. The watch's loss of time in one position is cancelled out by the gains it makes in the opposite position. This mechanism is extremely delicate and considered to be one of the most ingenious inventions in the history of horology.

TRITIUM: a phosphorescent substance that, when applied to hour markers and hands, makes it possible to read the time in the dark.

TROTTEUSE: a French term used internationally to designate the large chronograph hand.

TUNING FORK: an electronic movement regulated by a small tuning fork. The vibrations of the tuning fork are extremely stable and thus guarantee the watch a considerable degree of precision.

ULTRA-THIN: an extremely thin case or movement.

VIBRATION: the movement of the balance from one extreme to the other. Watches are also distinguished based on the number of vibrations their movements make per hour, vph (sometimes expressed with the abbreviation A/h, standing for "alterations per hour"). For wristwatches, the most common vph are: 18,000, 19,800, 21,600, 28,800 and 36,000. In theory, construction precision being equal, the higher the number of vph, the more accurate the watch.

WATCH CRYSTAL: a transparent piece set into the bezel to protect the watch dial or used in place of the watch back so that the movement can be observed. In horology, various materials are used to make watch crystals: acrylic (an unbreakable plastic material), mineral glass (ordinary tempered glass with a good degree of resistance) and sapphire glass (made of synthetic corundum and difficult to scratch).

WATER-RESISTANCE: the capacity of a case to resist water infiltration, expressed in atmospheres (atm).

WHEEL TRAIN:

the component that transmits power in mechanical watches, comprising a series of dentelated wheels interlocked such that each wheel turns at a speed exactly proportional to that of the wheel before and after it.

WHEEL: in horology, wheels are dentelated components that transmit motion. They are part of wheel trains, trains and mechanisms, and are distinguished based on shape, position and function.

WORLD TIME:

a watch that indicates multiple time zones on a chapter ring marked with the key cities linked to the twenty-four time zones.

Bibliography

BARRACCA J., NEGRETTI G., NENCINI F., *Le temps de Cartier*, Wrist 1989

BERNER G.-A., *Dictionnaire professionnel illustré de l'horlogerie*, Chambre Suisse de l'Horlogerie 1996

BORER A., *Richard Mille*, Cercle d'Art 2006

BRANDT P., *Ulysse Nardin. History In Time*, Argò 1996

BREGUET E., *Breguet: horloger depuis 1775. Vie et postérité d'Abraham-Louis Breguet, 1747–1823*, Alain de Gourcuff 1997

BRUNNER G., PFEIFFER-BELLI CH., *Wristwatches*, Könemann 1999

BRUNNER G., *Heuer–Tag Heuer. Mastering Time*, Assouline 1997

BRUNNER G.L., PFEIFFER BELLI CH., *Eterna. Pioneers In Watchmaking*, Eterna 2006

BRUNNER G.L., PFEIFFER-BELLI CH., WEHRLI M.K., *Audemars Piguet: Masterpieces of Classical Watching*, Audemars Piguet 1993

BRUSA G., *L'arte dell'orologeria in Europa*, Bramante Editrice 1978

BRUTON E., *The History of Clocks & Watches*, Chartwell Books 2004

CARCANO L., CEPPI C., *L'alta orologeria in Italia. Strategie competitive nei beni di prestigio*, Egea 2006

CARRERA R., *Swatchissimo*, Antiquorum 1991

CHAILLE F., *Girard-Perregaux*, Flammarion 2004

CIPOLLA C.M., *Clocks and Culture, 1300–1700*, Norton 1978

COLOGNI F., NEGRETTI G., NENCINI F., *Piaget: Watches and Wonders Since 1874*, Abbeville Press, 1996

COLOGNI F., *Jaeger-Lecoultre. The Story of the Grande Maison*, Flammarion 2006

COLOGNI F., *The Secrets of Vacheron Constantin: 250 Years of History*, Flammarion 2005

DANIELS G., *Art of Breguet*, Sotheby Parke Bernet 1981

DANIELS G., *Watchmaking*, Sotheby's 1981

DE VECCHI P., GREGATO G., *Patek Philippe. Complicated Wrist Watches*, Konemann 1999

DE VECCHI P., NEGRETTI G., *Orologi*, Fabbri–Rizzoli Grandi Opere 1993

DE VECCHI P., UGLIETTI A., *Orologi da polso*, Istituto Geografico De Agostini 2000

DOWLING J.M., HESS J.P., *Rolex Wristwatches. An Unauthorized History*, Schiffer Publishing 1996

FALLET E., *Tissot: 150 Years of History 1853–2003*, Tissot 2003

FLÉCHON D., *The Mastery Of Time*, Flammarion–FHH 2011

FRITZ M., *Reverso: The Living Legend*, Braus/Jaeger-LeCoultre 1992

GENOUD H., *Breitling. The Book*, Breitling 2009

GOBBI P., *I cronografi Rolex. La leggenda*, Sondep Editore 2004

HUBER M., BANBERY A., *Patek Philippe*, Patek Philippe/Antiquorum 1998

ISNARDI A., *The Master of Omega*, GTime s.d. 2006

Kahlert H., Muhe R., Brunner G.L., *Wristwatches: History of a Century's Development*, Schiffer Pub Ltd 2004, 5th rev. ed.

Lambelet C., Coen L., *World of Vacheron Constantin Geneve*, Edizioni Scriptar/Vacheron Constantin 1992

Landes D., *Revolution in Time: Clocks and the Making of the Modern World*, Belknap Press 1983

Lang G., Meis R., *Chronograph Wristwatches*, Schiffer Pub Ltd, 1997

Meis R., *A. Lange & Sohne. Great Timepieces from Saxony*, Lange Uhren GmbH, 2012

Meis R., *Pocket Watches: From the Pendant Watch to the Tourbillon*, Schiffer Publishing 1987

Mella F.A., *La misura del tempo nel tempo*, Ulrico Hoepli Editore 1990

Mondani F., Mondani G., *1908–2008: 100 Years of Rolex*, Guido Mondani Editore 2008

Morozzi D., Toselli G., *Longines*, Edizioni Giada 1990

Negretti G., De Bruton S., *Panerai*, Flammarion 2008

Negretti G., *Legendary Watches: Officine Panerai*, Publiprom 1998

Negretti G., *Panerai Historia: From the Depths of the Sea*, Officine Panerai 1999

Nencini F., Negretti G., *I signori del tempo*, Editoriale Wrist/Technimedia 1986

Nencini F., Negretti G., *Ore d'oro [Wrist Watches: Investment and Passion]*, Editoriale Wrist/Technimedia 1984

Paci M., Zei D., *Panerai Watches from 1936 to 1997 and Panerai in Florence: 150 Years of History*, Patrizzi & Co. 2009

Patrizzi M., Patrizzi O., *Collezionare orologi da polso*, Guido Mondani Editore/Antiquorum 2002

Patrizzi M., Patrizzi O., *Collezionare orologi Patek Philippe–Collecting Patek Philippe Watches*, Guido Mondani Editore/Antiquorum 2004

Patrizzi O., *Collezionare orologi da polso Rolex*, Guido Mondani Editore 2001

Patrizzi O., *Dictionnaire des horlogers genevois*, Antiquorum 1998

Pozzoli M., *Nozioni di orologeria*, Loescher Editore 1957

Pritchard K.H., *Swiss Masterpiece Makers*, Phoenix Publishing 1997

Richon M., *Omega Saga*, Fondation Adrien Brandt en faveur du patrimoine Omega 1998

Richon M., *Omega. A Journey Through Time*, Omega 2007

Richter B., *Breitling. The History of a Great Brand of Watches 1884 to Present*, Schiffer Publishing Ltd. 2000

Tolke H., King J., *IWC, International Watch Co., Schaffhausen*, Ineichen 1986

Veroni A., *Hublot: The Watch of Royalty*, Argò Editore 2001

Von Osterhausen F., *The Movado History*, Schiffer Publishing 1996

ACKNOWLEDGEMENTS
The authors would like to thank the press offices of the various horology houses, Ivo Bernardi, Fabio Bertini, Letizia Briccolani, Maria Cherubini, Nicola de' Toma, Carlo Fontana, Giorgio Gregato, Enrico Mazzola, Giorgia Murano, Giampiero Negretti, Walter Pavanello, Ileana Pisa, Maristella Pisa, Paola Pujia, Augusto Veroni and Lorenzina Vittori.